READ WHAT OTHER PEOPLE ARE SAYING ABOUT MARK EVAN DM,DN'S VIRTUAL REAL ESTATE INVESTING MADE EASY...

"The information contained on page 101 alone is worth 1,000 times the price of the book. That one page allowed me to make more money on one deal than I did in 3 months at my full-time job! Thanks for sharing this with us."

- Jeremy Blunt

"I just wanted to thank you for sharing the ideas in your virtual real estate system. Also, thank you for taking time out of your busy schedule to meet with Nicole and I in Baltimore. From that single meeting, you helped us fix our posture when talking to sellers. Now we only deal with the sellers that NEED to sell not want to sell. We are pre-screening sellers at lightning-speed now. Invariably, that has allowed us to talk to more sellers, which, in turn, allows us to make more offers, which leads to more deals. I look forward to my next meeting where I can view first hand how to automate your system."

- Haydn Hislop

This book is a must read for anyone who wants to make consistent money in the new real estate market. Chapter 4 alone has saved me thousands of dollars and months of time in setting up my virtual real estate business. This book explains every detail and lays out every step you need to making a fortune through virtual real estate investing. Awesome stuff, thanks again Mark."

- David Geisler

READ WHAT OTHER PEOPLE ARE SAYING ABOUT MARK EVAN DM,DN'S VIRTUAL REAL ESTATE INVESTING MADE EASY...

This is a great book to learn how to become a virtual real estate investor. These are the same lessons that allowed me to do deals and get my business rolling. I really can't say enough about Mark Evans DM. He has helped me in so many ways to get my business going in the right direction. The tools are here in this book to help you become virtual. Sometimes, taking that first step is the most difficult to do. Taking action is the crucial part. Then continue to implement and keep moving forward to success.

- Rosanne Cellini

"I once thought that real estate investing was an opportunity only for those with deep pockets or for those who wanted to put up with the hassle of late night phone calls from tenants with clogged toilets. But The DM introduced me to his real estate investing system that doesn't require deep pockets and will keep my phone from ringing off the hook. I'm following this book step-by-step (as I write this, I'm doing the work described in chapter 4). I've learned that my own success in real estate has more to do with my level of action than getting everything perfect 100% of the time. Thanks for making it so easy, Mark! I'm taking massive action!"

- Aaron Hoos

Virtual Real Estate Investing Made Easy

How to Quit Your Job and Make Fast Cash
Wholesaling Real Estate

By Mark Evans DM,DN

Mark Evans DM,DN
Virtual Real Estate Investing Made Easy: How to Quit Your Job
and Make Fast Cash Wholesaling Real Estate

ISBN 978-0-9788170-4-6

Publisher: Deal Maker Publishing LLC

Note:

- The forms provided in this book are *examples* of the forms used by real estate investors. However, each state has its own legal requirements. Have an attorney review all forms before using them.
- Remember to do your due diligence before starting any business venture and prior to investing in any type of investment.

DEDICATION

This book is dedicated to YOU, the reader. Without you, these words are merely words. But with you implementing these words in your business, you will grow a real estate investing business that most will only dream of. So I am dedicating this book to all those who will take this book and implement what you learn here. Go for your dreams! More importantly, live your dreams.

And

This book is also dedicated to my 5 beautiful nieces (in the order of oldest to youngest…) Payton, Samantha, Roslyn, Kadyn, Kyndall. You have such an awesome opportunity in today's world! You're the next generation of wealth – the information generation – and the opportunities available to you are literally unlimited! You're in charge of your future and you can achieve even more in your lives than most of us could ever dream.

And

This book is also dedicated to my parents, Mark and Sandy. You gave me life and have supported me in everything. Your showing up means so much to me. Thank you!

And

This book is also dedicated to Deena, my fiancé and travel partner. What would I do without you? You make me want to travel farther and reach higher because you're there beside me.

"Every second on the clock is a moment of choice: You can choose to take action and grow or you can choose not to. Those who achieve their goals are the ones who chose to take action"

- The DM

TABLE OF CONTENTS

DISCLAIMER

Money Isn't Falling From The Sky

I've packed this book with useful information about building a virtual real estate investing business.

But here's the deal: The results I describe aren't typical. I can only show you what I've achieved and how I did it.

If you're reading this and wondering why money isn't falling from the sky then you've missed a critical point that I try to make over and over: Most people gather information but they let it grow dusty on the shelves.

Here's The One Secret That Successful People Know

The most successful people in the world learn, plan, and then they take relentless, massive action. They move forward with a disciplined attitude and they accept the challenges and hard work required.

Remember: If achieving goals were easy, everyone would be doing it. So read this book and then put it into practice and keep working relentlessly toward your dreams.

-The DM,DN

"Few things are impossible to diligence and skill. Great works are performed not by strength, but perseverance"

- Samuel Johnson

PROLOGUE #1

HOW THIS BOOK WILL (OR WON'T)
CHANGE YOUR LIFE

Buyer Beware! This Book Won't Make You Rich.

Let's get one thing out of the way before you start reading: This book WON'T make you rich or successful. That might be a little shocking to read, so let me explain...

In this book, you're going to read about financial freedom and about success and about money... and how virtual real estate investing can help achieve those things.

But we all define those terms differently. I can't look into your life, see your situation with perfect clarity, and give you the exact advice you need to be successful. (In fact, I'm not even sure how you define those terms... because we each define them slightly differently).

Rather, the only thing I can do in this book is give you the vision and the tools and the steps that have helped to make me successful. I can show you what I do (and what I'd do if I were you) to enjoy the freedom and lifestyle that comes from virtual real estate investing.

The rest is up to you.

Why I'm Like An Airplane (And So Are You)

Before you start, there are a few important things to point out (that are sometimes missed) so I want to put them front-and-center for you to read:

First, when I describe the steps and processes and tools I use in virtual real estate investing, please be aware that I'm sharing

13

with you what has worked for me. You'll read about these steps and processes and tools but before you put them into action, think for yourself about whether or not they are appropriate for you (or whether you have a different set of skills, resources, or strengths that might allow you to achieve the same result in a different way.

And very important: Be sure to get educated about how to do these things effectively for your situation. In particular, you should be aware of the laws where you will be running your business in order to protect yourself and make sure you are compliant with the law.

Second, it is critical to understand that I'm painting a big picture here, and my perspective (as someone who has been real estate investing for a while) will be different than yours. You will need to do a bit of work in order to achieve the level I'm working at, and in order to get to the same big picture.

What I mean is: If my business and your business are airplanes, I'm running a 747 at 35,000 feet and your business (which is presumably just getting started) is a small prop plane speeding down the runway. So in writing this book, I'm giving you the steps and processes and tools to become successful in virtual real estate investing but it's not always an automatic flip-the-switch opportunity. I'm giving you a view from 35,000 feet. You may need to do a bit of work to get your business into the air.

However, the big picture I'm painting is intended to show you what to work toward. And as someone who has done the work and built a real estate investing business that operates virtually, I can give you this advice: Put in the time, do the work, and (sooner than you realize) you can build your own virtual real estate investing business.

PROLOGUE #2

WHY I WROTE THIS BOOK

Many People Are Scared Of This One Thing

Every time you turn on the TV or pick up the newspaper, you can't help but see bad news everywhere – whether it's the economic crisis in Europe, or the faltering economy in the US, or the economic uncertainty elsewhere in the world.

It seems like everyone is worried about what could happen to the financial world tomorrow. As I write this, it really feels like the world is just teetering on the brink of financial apocalypse.

To most people, it can feel scary. In all of this uncertainty, people tend to take fewer risks. They adopt a "bunker" mentality where they just want to keep their head down and work at their regular 9-5 jobs and pay their bills and hope that the next wave of pink slips and foreclosures pass over them and hit somewhere else.

But even though people are fearful because of the global economic crisis, they still dream of living a lifestyle they want to live (to take nice vacations or own a nicer home or send the kids to a good college). Working that 9-5 job isn't going to help achieve those goals. Most people know that some change is necessary if they are going to achieve their dreams and goals in life. However, many people are scared to death of making the necessary changes when everything feels so uncertain.

People Are Scared, But They Know This One Truth

In every crisis there is opportunity and history shows us again and again that the most successful people are the ones who took a chance on something that the rest of the world overlooked because of that bunker mentality.

So, there is a crisis right now in the financial markets (and that has an impact on the real estate markets). Foreclosures are high. Buying is down.

But there is also opportunity! The most obvious opportunity is the opportunity to buy low-priced properties and then rent them out. Another popular opportunity (that is frequently shown on TV) is rehabbing or flipping, where you buy a low-priced home and you fix it up and resell it.

I have done those kinds of investing and there's nothing wrong with them except that they can be hard work and, of course, it takes money. And it can be pretty hands-on and work-intensive.

There Is a Faster, Easier Way to Invest In Real Estate

There's nothing wrong with being a landlord and renting out properties but that kind of real estate investing can keep you really busy.

As you'll learn later in this book, I wanted to be successful but I didn't want to work hard on an ongoing basis for it. (Rather, I wanted to work hard once, to set-up my business, so that my real estate business would run without me constantly working in it every day).

But being a landlord is not the only way that you can invest in real estate. I'm going to show you a way to become a real estate investor that doesn't require your own money and that doesn't require a lot of time.

It's possible you've never heard of this investing method before but it is an exciting way to make money. And the best part is: You don't need to do it by sitting at your desk answering phones all day long.

In this book, I'm going to show you exactly what this real estate investing system is and how you can start and grow your own virtual real estate investing business.

"The bravest thing you can do when you are not brave is to profess courage and act accordingly."

- Corra Harris

"No one decides to procrastinate. It just happens. The only way to fight it is to act, and the best time to fight it is right now. If not now... When???"

- The DM

INTRODUCTION

Get Inspired... By Your Dreams

Before I reveal all of my virtual real estate investing secrets, I want to tell you briefly about my life – to show you where I came from and where I am today.

I don't tell you these things to impress you but to impress upon you just how powerful and effective the techniques are that I'll be describing in this book. I hope to tell you a little about my life to inspire you and get you excited about the possibilities.

And although I'm currently living what I define as my ideal lifestyle, please remember that your ideal lifestyle might be different. Your end-goals don't have to be the same as mine (and a virtual real estate investing business can help you achieve your goals... whatever they are).

So I hope to inspire you but I hope you are also inspired by your own dreams – learn from these pages to help you live the life you want to live.

I've Come A Long Way

I'm writing these words from a beautiful rented condo overlooking the stunning scenery of Thailand. I just arrived here from Singapore. Earlier this year I spent almost two months in the Caribbean.

I'm on my second trip around the world – a 5 year trip that will also take my fiancé and me through several amazing countries in the Caribbean, Asia, and Europe.

In my first trip around the world, I toured the Caribbean and Europe, stopping at awe-inspiring places like Santorini,

Greece; Anguilla, British Virgin Islands; Maui, Hawaii; Paris, France; Venice, Italy; and Barcelona, Spain.

When people hear about the places I'm visiting on this round-the-world trip, or my last one, they wonder if I was born wealthy or won the lottery... or maybe a rich aunt willed me her huge estate when she passed away. But none of those things are true.

I was born into a hardworking lower-middle-class family in Midwestern America. My parents worked hard to provide for us but, by some people's standards, we didn't have much.

Like many other people from their generation, my parents came from the demographic of people who believe that the harder you work, the more successful you'll be. And although they were loving and positive to me, I sometimes wonder if they were secretly disappointed that I barely graduated from high school. Even though I always told them I was going to make a lot of money, they came from a generation that equated good grades with success... and I didn't have the good grades!

I've always wanted to be extremely successful – not only financially successful but also free to do what I want. I wanted to travel the world and not have to show up in an office or pick up a hammer.

I wanted freedom to do what I want, and I needed the money to do it. (This is often called "financial freedom", which means having the financial means to live the lifestyle you want without having to work for it).

The Curvy Road To Success

When I was first starting out, I thought I knew how to achieve those freedom goals. It took a few years (and a few failures and near bankruptcies) to find the right recipe to achieve what I wanted.

I learned something that seems to be very obvious, however many people don't know about it: Financial freedom doesn't come from a hard day's work at the office, where you get a paycheck at the end of the week and try to save a little each month for retirement.

That's the way many people work but it hasn't helped create wealthy people who retire early.

I learned that there is a different way to work – a way to work *smart*, not hard.

The DM explains...

When I say "work smart, not hard", I don't mean that you'll never work again. And, I'm not opposed to working hard, by the way. The key is: If you want to be financially free, you shouldn't work hard day-in and day-out to get paid only for the time you spend working hard. (That's the way most jobs are). Rather, I want to work hard once and get paid forever for that work. That's the secret to achieve success. Working hard means showing up to work and grinding out your work every single day. Working smart means building a business of systems that will run almost by themselves (with very little input from you).So, "working smart, not hard" means building a business that is almost completely automated. And, "working smart, not hard" allows you to work hard once to start up your business and then run your business from anywhere once it is up and running. I'll talk more about this throughout the book.

If you knew me when I was a kid, you'd never believe that I'd get where I am today – up here at the top of a beautiful condo overlooking a jaw-dropping vista. I want to share with you how I did it and how it's possible for you to do it too.

Over the years, I've tried to give back in various ways – by teaching and mentoring many others (just as I was mentored) and by writing five bestselling books and delivering webinars and seminars to thousands of people across the world to help people learn what I've learned.

And what I wanted to do in this book was to write down, in complete order, the simplest recipe I know to achieve the kind of success and financial freedom that I've achieved. You can piece together some of this stuff from my other books and webinars and blogs but I wanted to provide you with a complete end-to-end handbook that you could use to build your own virtual real estate investing business from anywhere in the world.

Of course, you don't have to go anywhere if traveling the world isn't your dream. This book isn't only for aspiring real estate investors who want to travel the world. This book is for aspiring real estate investors who want to be able to build a real estate investing business that doesn't require them to show up to the office by 8:00 AM every morning and work until 6:30 PM every night.

This book is really about having the freedom to do what you want when you want without having a job to tie you down and eat up most of your week. It's about having an income-producing real estate investing business that doesn't require you to lift a hammer or knock on your tenant's door to collect overdue rent. This book is about how to start and run – and succeed! – in real estate investing without you having to be present in your business every step of the way.

Want to take an extended vacation with your family without worrying about work piling up? No problem. Virtual wholesaling can help you afford to do that.

Want to go back to school and study something you always wished you learned? Want to easily pay for your kids' college education? No problem. Virtual wholesaling can help you afford to do that.

Want to give your parents a comfortable retirement that they deserve? No problem. Virtual wholesaling can help you afford to do that.

Want to travel the world like I do? No problem. Virtual wholesaling is how I have achieved my dream of traveling the world and it can help you do the same.

Yes, it is possible to achieve a life of freedom – financial and time freedom – to have the lifestyle that you want to have. I've built my real estate investing business to operate without me being present. I want to show you how.

The DM explains...

*I've mentioned this already but I want to mention it again here: I still run my business. I still work. This isn't one of those "never work again" scams that people sell. I'm not saying that you'll never have to work again. But there is a difference between working **in** your business and working **on** your business, and it's a difference that I'll revisit throughout this book. Working **in** your business is what you do when you do everything! You're answering phones, posting advertisements, and sweeping up like a janitor at the end of the day. Working **on** your business is a secret that the most successful business owners (in real estate investing and in other industries too) understand and adopt: Working on your business means setting up your business with a team and with technology and tools and other systems so that it can run automatically. Working on your business rather than working in your business is the same as working smart, not hard.*

It's Time To Dream About How Your Life Could Be...

The shortest distance between two points is a straight line. When I was growing up, I followed a curvy road to success, sometimes making mistakes along the way. I want to help you by showing you the fastest, most straightforward way to achieve the life you want to live.

So think of your life now and the life you want to live as two dots on a piece of paper, and think of this book as the ruler that will help you draw a straight line between the two dots. In other words, I'm helping you avoid the curvy road I took to get where I am today!

But I'm just a guide. I can only show you how to do something. It's up to you to do it. If you've ever been lost in an unfamiliar area of town and you stopped for directions, you probably got detailed directions and maybe even a map from someone who knew the area better than you. That's what this book is. It's the detailed directions and map. Now it's up to you to follow what I've written.

You might choose not to follow everything I've outlined – perhaps you want to go about your real estate investing business I a different way than what I've outlined here. That's fine, of course. But I'll show you the way that has worked for me and for many of my students and you could learn it and build on it to create your own success story. (And maybe someday you'll write a book of your own to guide people to their success!)

Are you ready to get started? Let's help you become a successful virtual wholesale investor to create the life you've always dreamed of.

Your friend and your proud mentor,

Mark Evans DM,DN

PART 1

VIRTUAL WHOLESALING AS AN OPPORTUNITY

In this part of the book, I'm going to introduce you to real estate investing and, specifically, to a type of real estate investing called "virtual wholesaling". I'll show you why I believe virtual wholesaling is the fastest, easiest way to achieve the freedom you need to live the life you want to live. If you set up your virtual wholesaling business correctly, you can quit your job and spend your time with your friends and family doing the things you love to do. Want to play golf all day? Want to hang out at the beach? Want to take your kids on a cross-country road trip? I'll show you why virtual wholesaling real estate can help you achieve that dream!

In this part of the book I'll also introduce you to some of the basic tools and systems you'll want to have to build a virtual wholesaling business so that it runs almost on autopilot (with very little input from you), earning you easy money while you spend your time doing whatever you want to do.

*"Keep away from people who try to belittle
your ambitions. Small people always do that,
but the really great make you feel that you, too,
can become great. "*

- Mark Twain

CHAPTER 1

HOW REAL ESTATE INVESTING CHANGED MY LIFE (AND HOW IT CAN CHANGE YOUR LIFE)

Maui, Hawaii, 6:28 PM
Writing from The Whaler

I'm sitting here with a couple new friends, sipping on Mai Tais and it hit me... this is real.

Here I am in another world (if you've ever been to Hawaii, you know what I mean) and while I'm sipping a Mai Tai and talking with someone I've only just met, I am making money. Right now. Automatically. I'm literally making money while I drink Mai Tais and listen to the crashing ocean surf.

And later, when I go for a quick evening swim in the ocean, I'm going to be making money then, too. And tomorrow, when I'm on the beach, I'm making money then, too.

It's still almost hard to believe... But it is real. I'm not sharing this with you to impress you but to impress upon you! I wish I knew what I'm about to share with you earlier in my career as it wasn't always like this.

What Is Success?

I'm on my second trip around the world. I live in villas, condos and house rentals, and I lay on beaches and enjoy the unique sights and sounds and foods of the different cultures of the places I visit.

Years ago, I decided that traveling the world was my idea of success. When I envisioned success, I envisioned myself traveling the world many times over.

Lots of people have a dream; an idea of success. They picture it in their minds and live it out in their imaginations. But most people put off their dreams and hope they can afford it during retirement. They simply don't think it's possible to live their idea of the perfect life right now.

Most people think of the perfect life as something to be lived in the future, once your working years are over. I didn't want to work until I could live my dreams. I wanted to live my dreams while I worked today.

What do you dream about for your life? My dream was to travel the world in first-class style. That might not be your dream. Maybe you want to move permanently to a tropical island or have enough money to pursue photography as a full-time hobby. I know one person who dreams of moving to the UK and someone else who dreams of being able to finally have the money and time to buy a classic car and restore it in their garage.

Your idea of a successful life probably includes some kind of activity or destination or key purchase. And implied (but never stated) in your dream is the need to have the money so that you don't have to work and so that you can fund this ideal lifestyle.

We call this "financial freedom". Financial freedom is a term that means you have enough money to do whatever you want. It means you have the money to live the successful life you're dreaming of.

To the concept of financial freedom, I also add the idea of "time freedom" – where you have enough time to enjoy hanging out with loved ones and to enjoy your pursuits.

The DM explains...

These concepts of financial freedom and time freedom are related because most people who achieve financial freedom have the money to quit their job (and now they have time freedom!). But I mention them here as two separate things because not everyone has both of them at the same time. An unemployed person might have time freedom but they don't

*have financial freedom to pursue their dreams.
And some wealthy people might have enough
money to be considered financially free but
they don't have the time freedom to pursue
their dreams because of other commitments.*

Financial freedom and time freedom are interrelated and when you achieve both, you can then start living what I call your ideal life.

I wouldn't be able to travel the world if it weren't for my own financial freedom and time freedom to do what I want.

The first requirement of success is that you have a definition for success – that you have a dream of your ideal life.

Once you know what you define as "the perfect lifestyle", achieving it is as simple as achieving the financial freedom and time freedom to pay for it and enjoy it.

So, this book is written to help you achieve your successful life – your dream life – by achieving financial freedom and time freedom, and I'm going to show you how it's possible to achieve this as a virtual wholesaling investor.

But first, we need to clear the air about the reason that most people don't achieve financial freedom, time freedom, and the success they dream of…

The Freedom Misconception

Many people have a dream of what their ideal life is and they can probably figure out that they need the financial freedom and time freedom to attain it.

They know they need financial freedom and time freedom. So why don't we see more people achieving those two freedoms and living the lifestyle of their choosing?

I believe the reason we don't see more people living their ideal dream life is because they have a critical misconception about how to achieve financial freedom and time freedom.

In short, people think they know how to achieve financial

freedom and time freedom but, quite frankly, they are wrong.

Here's the popular misconception: Most people believe that you need to show up and work hard and by doing those two things, you will achieve success.

From childhood, we're taught that our presence and our effort are necessary if we want to be successful. We have to show up to school and take tests and get good grades and go to college to ensure our successful lives.

And if we want to be successful in the workplace, we have to show up, sit at our desk, do what the boss says, and collect our paycheck each week, and save up little by little. And by showing up and working hard, we can succeed.

It doesn't work this way. If it did, more people would retire earlier in life and be living a lifestyle they want to live.

Instead, people show up to their job and punch the clock and do what their boss tells them to. They believe that all of this effort (plus some occasional savings put away into an IRA or 401(k)) will result in allowing them to live the life they want to live someday.

But for the majority of people, it just doesn't happen that way. For most people, you can't work your way to success by putting in extra hours at work and you can't save your way to wealth by putting aside a bit of money each month into your 401(k).

People go into debt to get a decent education and to own a decent home and a decent car and they don't earn enough from their decent job to pay for retirement. Most people are not going to be able to afford the lifestyle in their retirement that they've been putting off for their entire lives.

I don't want to live like that. And since you're reading this book, there's a good chance that you don't want that either. Like me, you probably want to start living your successful life before you retire, which means you need to achieve financial and time freedom now.

Showing up and working hard at a job (day-in and day-out for your entire adult life) aren't the secrets to achieving the financial freedom and time freedom we need to live the successful life we dream of.

So, if that isn't the answer to achieving success, what is? I'll go into detail later but the basic answer is ...

Achieve Financial Freedom And Time Freedom With Real Estate Investing

Everyone who wants to "save for the future" puts money into an IRA or a 401(k). They've been told about the benefit of investing and they want to enjoy those benefits to help make money to pay for their successful life *in retirement.*

Most people who know that they need to achieve financial freedom or time freedom to be successful will be told that investing will help them.

But there are a lot of different types of investments out there that can (in some circumstances) help you to make more money than you'd make at your job: Becoming self-employed is a type of investment. Investing in the stock market (through stocks or mutual funds) is a well-known type of investment. And investing in real estate is also type of investment.

Which should you choose?

I believe that real estate investing is the fastest and safest option to achieve financial freedom and time freedom. (In fact, I believe that a specific type of real estate investing called "Virtual Wholesaling" is a great place to start, but let's start with the basics.)

Let's look at each of the three types of investments I mentioned a moment earlier (self-employment, stock trading, and real estate investing) and later I'll show you why real estate investing is the most promising opportunity for you.

Self-employment: Self-employment is where you use your skills, talents, knowledge, and expertise to provide a product or service to a customer.

Self-employment might include starting up a roofing business or a freelance web design business or a hairdressing salon

– it's wide open!

The idea of becoming self-employed is very attractive because it leverages your background and education to allow you to make more money for yourself (instead of doing the same work as an employee and only earning a regular wage).

Stock trading: Stock trading is where you start with some money (often anywhere from $10,000 to $100,000) and you day trade or swing trade – trying to buy stocks as they go up and sell them before they go down.

Stock trading seems like a popular option because you don't have to deal with annoying bosses and customers, and there is software that automates the process. We've been led to believe that, at the click of a button, you can make thousands of dollars.

Real estate investing: Real estate investing is where you buy a property and then make money from a variety of exit strategies – you can rent it, lease it, or sell it. (There are many popular TV shows that show real estate investors flipping (buying a house, fixing it up, and trying to sell it). That's just one of many ways to invest in real estate. Again, stay tuned because I have some specific ways that I think are great strategies to invest your time in.

Real estate offers many different possibilities and because of today's shaky economy, there are even more lucrative possibilities.

All three of these options seem attractive to someone who wants to achieve financial freedom and time freedom because, unlike a job, there doesn't seem to be a cap on the money you can make from self-employment, stock trading, or real estate investing. Moreover, thanks to the internet, you can do these jobs from the comfort of your home very easily.

But the attractiveness is an illusion. Self-employment and stock trading, in my opinion, are far inferior to real estate investing (specifically, the virtual wholesaling concept that you're about to learn). Here's why:

- Self-employment and stock trading both require you to do daily work at your desk in order to be successful. With real estate investing (at least, the real estate investing I'm going to show you in this book), you don't need to be in an office or doing daily work in order to make money. (You'll still need to do some work but you can do it from anywhere).

- Self-employment and stock trading both require specialized knowledge (either of a particular skill that you'll sell or of a particular type of investment or sector that you're going to invest in). But with real estate investing, almost anyone with no educational background or expertise can achieve financial freedom and time freedom once you understand the fundamentals of the deals.

- Self-employment seems like it offers an unlimited income potential but it is limited – by the amount of time you have in a day. Many self-employment people have traded the 9-5 of their regular jobs for a longer day as self-employed entrepreneurs. On the other hand, real estate investing (especially virtual wholesaling) takes very little time when you follow a secret I'll show you in this book (Hint: You need to work on your business not in your business).

- Stock trading requires a relatively large amount of money to start off with. On the other hand, the real estate investing that you'll learn in this book requires almost no money at all. I started with no credit and no money at all so I'll tell you what I did. (We all start from different places, so get ready to learn how to create a virtual real estate empire!)

Can you see why I prefer virtual wholesaling? Compared to self-employment and stock trading, it doesn't require you to sit at your desk or in front of a computer to be successful, it's easier to get into, and it takes little money at all.

Now, some of you might be wondering – just what is virtual wholesaling and how does it differ from other types of real estate investing. And, how can it possibly help someone achieve financial freedom and time freedom now?

That's what I'll talk about in the next chapter so keep reading and get ready to be introduced to a powerful new opportunity in real estate investing that you might never have heard of before. This could be the secret that unlocks your dreams and allows you to achieve the ideal lifestyle you want to live now.

"Let me tell you the secret that has led me to my goal. My strength lies solely in my tenacity."

- Louis Pasteur

The DM's Action Steps From This Chapter

1. List everything you would do if you had the time to do it instead of having to show up to work every day. (i.e. Play with your kids, travel, read a book, etc.).

2. List everything you would do if you had the financial resources to do so. (i.e. Pay off your mortgage, travel, etc.)

3. Answer this question: What have you done lately to change your life? Is it making the difference you hope it's making?

4. List the fears and challenges you face in achieving the lifestyle you desire. (Hint: For most people, it's a lack of money and time as well as a fear of giving up the sense of stability that comes with a job. But there might be other factors holding you back). Keep this list handy because you'll use it again in future chapters.

*"Always bear in mind that your own resolution
to succeed is more important than any one
thing."*

- Abraham Lincoln

CHAPTER 2

DIFFERENT TYPES OF REAL ESTATE INVESTING (AND WHICH ONE I LIKE BEST)

Phi Phi Island, Thailand 8:12 AM
Writing from the beach

I'm listening to the waves crashing on the shore and weird birds chirping and I'm watching the sun creep up over the horizon. It's so peaceful here. This place is amazing.

As I sit here and enjoy the sunrise and the exotic sights and sounds, I can't help but think how different my life has become, thanks in part to one specific thing – real estate investing.

Yes, I'm the DM – the "Deal Maker" (because I make many kinds of deals) – but real estate investing has been key in allowing me to travel the world and visit places as diverse as Barcelona Spain and Phi Phi Island, Thailand.

But it hasn't always been like this. My earliest venture into real estate investing resulted in financial success but a significant time deficit. Traveling the world was a dream but it was the furthest thing from happening because of how much time I was spending on that venture.

I realized that if I wanted to fulfill my dreams and travel to these amazing places that many people will never even see in their lifetimes, I needed to make some changes... (scratch that...) major changes!

I'm going to show you how it's possible to invest in real estate so you have the freedom to do whatever you want to do in life.

The Best Kind of Real Estate Investing

One of the most frequent questions I'm asked by students I mentor is: "Hey DM, what's the best kind of real estate investing to get into?"

Real estate investing offers many opportunities, depending on your interests and skills and the amount of time and attention you want to spend on it. And although I believe that there is one type of real estate investing that has the potential to be the fastest and easiest way to achieve the dreams you have for your life, I'm not going to deny that there are people doing exciting things in other types of real estate investing.

When someone asks me what kind of real estate investing they should do, I tell them that I have my preferred systems (including what I describe in this book) but ultimately it comes down to this: "As long as you have a plan and your business is cash flow positive and allows you to achieve the success you want to achieve, go for it!"

I'm not promising anyone a life of being among the idle rich of the world. You should figure out what you consider to be your ideal life and then find a way to do it. I believe that it's achievable with the kind of real estate investing that I'll be talking about in this book. But I have to admit that not everyone is going to approach it in the same way with the same skills so you might have a different outcome and, in the end, prefer a different way to achieve your dreams.

Years from now, if you tell me that you ignored my advice and were still able to achieve all of the dreams you have in your life, I will still be happy for you and feel like I have accomplished something by educating you and encouraging you to find your own way.

But in this book, I'm going to show you one of the ways that I became known as The Godfather of Virtual Deal Making and achieved my dreams using a specific real estate investing technique called virtual wholesaling.

But before we get into what virtual wholesaling is, I want

to quickly make sure we're all on the same page when it comes to real estate investing in general, especially for my readers who are brand new to real estate investing. (Later, I'll go into detail about what virtual wholesaling is).

Different Types Of Real Estate Investing

There are many different types of real estate investing. You can buy a property, fix it up, and sell it (that's commonly called "flipping" or "rehabbing"). Or you can buy a large parcel of land, subdivide it, build a group of houses on the land, and then sell the houses individually. Or you can buy a property and rent it out.

There are many other types of real estate investing as well. The properties could be residential, commercial, industrial, agricultural – you name it!

So there are many types of real estate investors but in most cases, the real estate investor **buys a property** (or, in some cases, just **takes control of the property** without buying it), the investor **adds value** (by building or fixing the property, or simply by finding another real estate investor who wants to buy the property for more money) and **then makes money** from that property (by selling or renting the property, or by assigning the contract to another investor who will buy the property).

You've probably heard of some of these, which are just a few of the different types of real estate investing techniques out there:

- Development

- Flipping

- Preconstruction investing

- Subject-To investing

- Rehabbing

- Short sale investing

- Pre-foreclosure investing

- Wholesaling

Perhaps you've heard of others.

There are experts and gurus who have done well in each of these types of real estate investing, and as you have probably noted, flipping is among the most famous types of real estate investing because it gets a lot of airtime on TV. But of all the types of real estate investing out there, I have one favorite type that I enjoy because I can do it from anywhere.

There are advantages and disadvantages to each kind of real estate investing. But I want to tell you about virtual wholesaling because I believe it's the fastest, easiest way to make the money you want to achieve the lifestyle you want to live.

I like virtual wholesaling because it's virtual – that is, it can be done from anywhere without the kind of effort that the other real estate investing techniques require.

I've been called the Godfather of Virtual Deal Making (specifically Virtual Wholesaling) because even though I do other types of deals – in real estate and in other business ventures – I almost only do deals that can be done virtually from anywhere in the world without requiring me to be on the phone or face-to-face with the seller or rehabbing a house with a hammer in one hand.

In this book, I'll describe how I run a virtual wholesaling real estate business from anywhere in the world.

The DM explains…

As I mentioned, I'm describing how I run a virtual wholesaling real estate business from anywhere in the world. I'll show you the exact steps and systems I use. And for someone who wants to start a real estate business, you can follow these steps. But some of you might already have a real estate investing business, or you don't dream of traveling the world and you want to be a little more hands-on in your business. You can still follow the steps in this book and just customize the ideas for your goals. I'm writing this book with the goal to make every reader a virtual investor so that you have the freedom in life to do what you want.

So, let's answer the one burning question you are probably asking me right now:

What Is Virtual Wholesaling?

Although I'll go into greater detail in the book, I want to first give you a very brief overview of what virtual wholesaling is here. I'll build on this definition throughout the rest of the book because many think they know what it is but I have seen many holes in their thoughts. I want to fully equip you to be a virtual wholesaler and the first step is to clear the air and tell you exactly what a virtual wholesaler is and does.

(A great example of a common misconception among wholesalers is the requirement to use your own money. Virtual wholesaling doesn't require you to use your credit or your own money and yet, many people shy away from virtual wholesaling because they lump it in with other types of real estate investing that might require you to use your own credit or money).

A quick introduction to virtual wholesaling: Virtual wholesaling is when you tie up a property (again, without using any of your own money) and you make money from that property by assigning the contract (for a fee) to investor-buyers. And, you do it *virtually* (without meeting them face-to-face) using simple tools that are as easy-to-use as sending email or making a phone call.

It's called "virtual" wholesaling because you don't actually have to meet the seller or the buyer face-to-face and you can do it from anywhere in the world; and it's called virtual "wholesaling" because you make money by selling to investors instead of a person who will be the tenant or homeowner.

Why virtual wholesaling is the best opportunity for you to easily make fast cash without a lot of work: I'll explain in a little more detail in a moment but I want to highlight a couple of things:

- Virtual wholesaling is one of the simplest forms of real estate investing because you're not building anything or navigating a lot of local government bureaucracy (unlike a property developer who has to fight every step of the way to get permits to build on a piece of land).

- Virtual wholesaling eliminates the need for you to use any of your own money or credit to do a deal (if you do it the way I do it, anyways). So this is a great type of real estate investing to get into even if you barely have a penny to your name! In fact, you don't need credit because you won't be taking out a loan in your name.

- Virtual wholesaling can be almost entirely automated so you can minimize any work you need to do. Many people who are starting out as virtual wholesalers are surprised at how little work there is to do! Here's what I mean: Just like other businesses, real estate investing does have different activities that need to be accomplished in order to invest successfully. However, what makes virtual wholesaling different from other businesses and real estate investing techniques is that it can be automated (I'll show you how a little later in the book). That's why I'm able to spend so much time at the beach or walking through exotic local markets or sailing down a canal in Venice with my fiancé Deena.

- Virtual wholesaling can be done virtually – online! – from anywhere in the world, giving you the freedom to run your real estate investing business from bed or your back deck or your favorite coffee shop or your vacation home or the beach (or, in my case: Spain or Greece or Italy or France or India or Thailand or the Caribbean or the Czech Republic!).

- Virtual wholesaling can be lucrative. Although everyone will have a different outcome (dependent on a number of factors, of course), it is possible to earn a significant income that you don't have to work at a job… that's what virtual wholesaling has done for me and that's what I want to show you in this book.

Virtual wholesaling is a huge opportunity for you to achieve the time-freedom and financial-freedom you need to do whatever you want to do in life.

Virtual wholesaling in more detail: So now that I have told you some of my favorite benefits of virtual wholesaling, I want to return to my earlier brief definition of virtual wholesaling and go into it in a bit more detail. As I explain it further, you'll see how these great benefits are built right in to virtual wholesaling:

1. Using simple, automated marketing (that requires almost no effort from you), you attract sellers who are interested in having someone buy their property. You take control of the property with a Letter of Intent (LOI), which gives you time to review the property.

2. After you've had a chance to review the property to decide if it's a property you want to move forward on (this process is automated, by the way, and requires very little time at all from you), you negotiate with the seller to establish terms on the property. (Note: You don't actually buy the property, simply establish the terms. Keep reading to find out why).

3. Once the terms have been established, you sign an Option to Purchase, which tells the seller that you (*or someone you assign the property to* – that's the important part) can purchase the property from them at an agreed price. You do need to cut a check for a small amount (between $1.00 and $10.00) to make this a legal binding contract. But that's the only amount you'll need to spend.

4. Using simple automated tools (again, I'll show you how), you offer the opportunity to your investor-buyers to purchase the deal: For a fee, you assign the Option to Purchase to your investor-buyer. (Notice how the property itself isn't bought or sold yet. Rather, you simply sell the investor-buyer the opportunity to buy the property!)

5. The investor-buyer closes the deal with the seller using their own money to buy the property and to do whatever they want with it (i.e., rent it, rehab it, whatever).

That's the wholesaling process. It's simple and virtual; it requires almost no ongoing work from you (just a few steps to set everything up – I'll show you how in this book).

The DM explains…
Every business offers its customers value. McDonald's offers its customers the ability to buy fast food. General Motors offers its customers the ability to buy a reliable American-made car. In a similar way, you are running a business – a real estate business – and your investor-buyers are kind of like your customers. So what value do you offer your investor-buyers? It's simple: They want to buy a property (perhaps to sell or to rent) and you find those deals and negotiate a good price with the seller.

Most importantly, it requires none of your own credit or money for you to make money! None of the steps in the example above requires any money from you (other than maybe $1.00 to $10.00 to make the contract a legal binding contract... and if $10 bucks is going to break you then real estate investing probably isn't for you... and or you could take on a partner for the 10 bucks and pay them back when you close). So if you do spend thousands of your own dollars, you are doing the system wrong!

Virtual Wholesaling Versus Rehabbing

Before going into greater detail about virtual wholesaling, I want to pause a moment and compare virtual wholesaling to rehabbing

Rehabbing (sometimes called "flipping") is SO popular right now and there seems to be a flipping show on every channel on television. And brand new investors look at the dollar signs that they think are being made in flipping and it's easy for them to think that flipping is the best, most lucrative type of real estate investing out there.

With flipping, you buy a property (usually at a discount because it's in rough shape) and you fix it up and sell it. On TV, it all happens over the course of a 30- or 60-minute episode and there are usually some hilarious nonsense and well-placed drama in between the commercial breaks... and at the end of the episode viewers are wowed with the big profits that are *potentially* earned on the homes.

But there are a few problems with flipping that I don't like, which are solved by virtual wholesaling:

Problem number 1: Flipping a property is largely dependent on the market. Buying low is possible and selling high is possible but not always in the same neighborhood in a short period of time.

On the other hand, virtual wholesaling has none of these problems. You don't have to worry about timing the market to buy low and sell high. You don't have to worry about the neighborhood. You don't have to worry about the economy. You're earning a fee by finding a deal that another investor-buyer wants to buy. This model, by the way, works in every neighborhood, whether it's an area full of really cheap properties or whether it's an area with ultra-high-end homes. And, of course, anything in between.

Problem number 2: There is no cash flow in flipping. You tie up your capital to buy a property and then you tie up more capital to fix it up. You get these big spikes in income (*if* you sell the property) but that's not cash flow and it's hard to plan for because a property might sell within a few days of your completed flip or it might not sell for weeks... or even months.

46

That's another benefit of virtual real estate investing over flipping: You don't have to tie up your capital to buy and repair the property. With virtual wholesaling, you don't have to spend ANY of your own money to invest. (I'll show you how! It's easier than you think).

And with virtual wholesaling, there is an unconventional way to generate cash flow if you set it up correctly (I'll show you how in the chapter on advanced techniques later in this book!).

Problem number 3: Flipping is hard work! There is a lot of blood and sweat that go into a successful flip – it's dirty, dusty, smelly work. That might appeal to some people but in my ideal world, the only dirt in my life is the sand between my toes on a sunny beach!

Virtual wholesaling doesn't have any of that work. I haven't lifted a hammer in years. I haven't demolished a house in years. I haven't hung drywall or plastered or painted or hauled lumber for years. I'm a real estate investor who rarely even steps foot inside my properties (and yet, I control a pretty big, very profitable business with a bunch of properties). I know many reading this will go against my advice here but if you have NO experience at all in rehabbing, I'd recommend you stay far as way from wanting to buy and rehab a house. Do this when you have a ton of money in the bank and you can do it as a hobby, not a business. However if you're a contractor who has experience in this sort of thing, this is a good way to invest (as long as you are working on your business instead of in your business)

Problem number 4: My biggest issue with flipping comes from my own experience. I used to flip houses when I first started real estate investing. I didn't want a job so I started real estate investing. The problem is I was working longer hours than I would have if I had a job! Flipping is more-than-full-time work and I've never met a flipper who got into the business because they wanted to work MORE hours!

With virtual wholesaling, the emphasis is on setting up your real estate investing business in a very specific way to succeed... WITHOUT requiring you to be at your desk or glued to your telephone or sanding a hardwood floor.

Here's Where Most Real Estate Investors Get It Wrong

I hope I've started to convince you that virtual wholesaling is not only possible, it's the best choice for an investor who wants to achieve the financial and time freedom to pursue their dreams.

But I'm going to make a bold (and even slightly depressing) prediction based on my experience:

Many people will read this book and get excited about the possibility. And when they put down the book, many people will forget the lessons they've learned here and they will run out and try to flip a house.

Why?

Because most of us are conditioned that we need to show up and work hard to succeed... and the more we show up and work hard, the more likely we will be to succeed. And that mindset is not only instilled by schools and parents and portraits of success, it's also supported by the flipping shows that dominate the airwaves.

So I will say this, which might shock you: With a very small exception of people, most of the people who flip real estate are just trading a day-job for a different day-job that has a lot of risks and A LOT of work for the reward.

I hope by now you agree: There are many types of real estate investing strategies out there but the best way to invest should be the type of investing that has the potential to allow you to achieve whatever you dream for your life. And for most people, that doesn't include the blood, sweat, and tears and 18-hour days of an unpredictable flip. Instead, the fastest, easiest way to enjoy the freedom you want in your life is through virtual wholesaling.

Keep reading! In the next chapter, I'm going to answer the question you're probably asking right now: "How do I run a virtual wholesaling business?"

The DM's Action Steps From This Chapter

1. Write down what you know about wholesaling. (Don't worry if it's right or wrong. I'll tell you more about it in a future chapter but this is a valuable teaching tool for you to articulate your "starting point").

2. Commit to taking action. If you are serious about becoming a virtual wholesaling real estate investor, promise yourself that you'll take action, right now!

3. Review the lists you made from the Action Steps in chapter 1 to remind yourself of the activities you'd do if you had the time and the financial resources to do whatever you desire.

"No great man ever complains of want of opportunity."

- Ralph Waldo Emerson

"The secret to success in business isn't really a secret at all: Find a system that works then get the system working for you. People try to make it more complicated than that but it doesn't have to be."

- The DM

CHAPTER 3

"HEY DM, HOW DO YOU RUN A BUSINESS WITHOUT BEING IN THE DRIVER'S SEAT?"

Barcelona, Spain 3:27 PM
Writing from a cafe

These old European cities have so much history in their narrow, twisting streets. The cities are old but there is so much bustling activity. It's entertaining to watch. I'm writing this from a little café on a narrow street. Deena will be joining me shortly, following an afternoon of shopping.

I'm sipping my cappuccino and watching the people go by. Life is pretty good! If you would've known me then you'd say I was set to be working hard for life.

But from my seat in this outdoor café, I can't help but think that I have surpassed even the careers that people consider "successful" ones. Those doctors and lawyers still have to fight traffic to show up to their hospitals and courtrooms on time every day; they work long hours; and go home only to do it all over again the next day. We call those work-intensive careers a success? (Note: Of course I'm thankful for these folks. We all need doctors! I just mean: If you want time freedom and financial freedom, don't become a doctor or a lawyer because these professions work very hard).

On the other hand, I'm sitting at an outdoor café on another continent, drinking a very strong cappuccino. It's like I'm on a permanent vacation because my business has been set up to be almost completely hands off. Don't get me wrong: I run my business. But I learned that running my business doesn't mean that I have to be in an office.

How Most Real Estate Investors Get It Wrong

Starting a business takes a lot of work and many entrepreneurs who build their start-ups work round-the-clock for months and even years to get their business running.

Aspiring real estate investors have bought into that thinking, too! I think it's partly because we see stories of those huge windfall deals from real estate flippers on TV (and they seem to be working around the clock) and it's also partly because we've been led to believe that success is directly linked to showing up and working hard.

So these real estate investors trade in their 9-5 day-jobs for a career as a real estate investor, only to find themselves busier than ever, working longer hours and sometimes with less money to show for their efforts at the end of the week!

These real estate investors end up measuring success by how often their phone rings and how many hours of the day they end up working. Soon, their entire lives orbit each deal. I used to live on that planet!

That doesn't sound like a dream life to me! As I talked about in chapter one, that's not the kind of life I want to live (although there was a time very early in my career when even I bought into that thinking too! Fortunately, I realized it wasn't how I wanted to live my life and I did something about it… and I'm showing you how you can, too).

Although real estate investing is fun, I'm sure you also have other things in life you'd like to achieve. I know I did, which is why I changed my life and am writing this book to you today.

You have dreams and goals and a vision for your ideal life and you want real estate investing to get you there, not to BE the end-result! Your dream of an ideal life (hopefully) does not include you tied to your desk with your phone cord.

Although making real estate deals is a lot of fun, there are other things in life – family, friends, a nice cottage, a warm beach, a good book, an extended vacation, playing with your kids, enjoying your hobbies, you name it!

But because our default mindset is that success is directly

linked to showing up and working hard, it's easy for many aspiring real estate investors to get caught up in that trap. And once you're in that trap, it's very hard to get out.

Here's The Truth That Successful People Will Tell You

As I've discussed in the previous chapters, success is not directly linked to showing up and working hard. Here's the real secret: **True success is directly linked to working smart.**

A real estate investing business DOES take work (I'm not denying that fact) but it doesn't mean that you should be tied to your desk or pulling shingles off of a roof for 12 to 16 hours a day.

Talking on your phone or hanging drywall in your rehab is working hard. It's not working smart.

Working smart is the secret that will help you run a real estate investing business that has the potential to give you the freedom you want in life.

Working smart means building your real estate investing business in such a way that it can run without you having to be present every moment of the day.

Working smart means building your real estate investing business to be something you can handle minimally by phone, email, fax or FedEx.

Working smart means changing your mindset about what your real estate investing business does and how you do it.

And most importantly, working smart means changing your mindset about what you consider to be an important and valuable use of your time.

I'm not the only one who talks about the difference between working hard and working smart:

- Michael E. Gerber of *The E-Myth* books (who I had the privilege of interviewing as part of my first book!) makes the distinction between Entrepreneur-Leaders who do leadership work and Managers and Technicians who do the hands-on work. Too many real estate investors are not working smart by doing the leadership work and are instead focusing on the hands-on work of managers and technicians.

- Robert Kiyosaki has a similar thing to say in his *Rich Dad* series. He gives a quadrant that describes employees and self-employed as people who work for their money while business owners and investors have their money work for them. Too many real estate investors think they are investors in Kiyosaki's quadrant but are really self-employed people who happen to be buying and selling real estate!

There are other experts who say a similar thing but one of my favorite ways of describing the difference between working hard and working smart is the distinction between working IN your business and working ON your business.

What It Means To Work ON Your Business (And Why It's Better)

Someone who works IN their real estate investing business works hard day-in and day-out to complete their work. They have to show up each day to their office or their property or they risk losing the deal and not making any money. These people are Michael Gerber's managers and technicians or Robert Kiyosaki's self-employed people. They are mastered by their business and their business would be dead in the water if they didn't answer the phone or pick up a hammer.

Someone who works ON their real estate investing business works smart to create a business that will run almost on its own – whether or not that person shows up to an office. These people are Michael Gerber's entrepreneur-leaders or Robert Kiyosaki's business owner/investors. They are the masters of their business and they have set up their business to run with only a little bit of attention.

The advantage of working ON your real estate investing business instead of in your business is simple:

When you set up your business so that it is not entirely dependent on you to show up and work hard, you have the freedom that I talked about in chapter one. You have a business that makes money whether or not you are sitting at your desk; you have a business that has the potential to provide you with the financial freedom and time freedom to live out your ideal lifestyle.

It's just a simple mindset change and it's not as strange as you might think. There are many jobs that illustrate the difference:

- In many businesses, the CEO isn't answering the phones or filing papers or dealing with customers; the workers are. Many real estate investors think of themselves as workers in their real estate investing business when they should instead think of themselves as CEOs. (By the way, there is nothing wrong with doing some of these pieces occasionally if they need to get done and someone else isn't available to do them. However, these activities shouldn't hinge on you doing them to be accomplished daily!)

- In Hollywood, the director tells the cast and crew what to do. The director themselves isn't also acting and filming and writing the script! Many real estate investors think of themselves as the entire cast and crew when they should instead be thinking of themselves as the director.

- In the military, the general isn't in the trenches

or driving a tank or fixing the engine on a helicopter. The general is looking at the big picture, leading and directing and telling others what to do. Many real estate investors see themselves as the general and the private!

- In government, the President isn't mowing the grass around town and deciding where to put street signs. Those things are left up to others while the President strategizes and plans and works at a higher level. Many real estate investors spend most of their time working on the lower-level work that they ignore or don't have time for the higher level work.

These other careers illustrate the difference between working IN your real estate investing business and working ON your business.

The DM explains...

The secret to working on your business instead of in your business is building systems. You identify all of the repeatable tasks and you build a system to complete those repeatable tasks for you so you don't have to do it yourself. It takes some work to set up initially but then you never have to do those repeatable tasks again! In the next section of this chapter, I'll show you how to build those systems.

How To Work On Your Real Estate Investing Business

There are two simple ways to work on your real estate investing business instead of in it: Automating and Outsourcing. I'll go into greater detail in the rest of the book about how to automate and how to outsource but I just want to touch in them here to define what I mean and to handle some of the initial questions you probably have:

- Automating is when you use technology and tools to have something done for you. One of the great things about virtual wholesaling is that there are a few really simple-to-use tools that you can use to effectively run a virtual business.

- Outsourcing is when you hire others to do some work for you. Again, one of the great things about virtual wholesaling is that there are a few different skills you can outsource to someone else, freeing up your time. (By the way, when I say "outsource" and "hire" I don't mean that you have a payroll or have to provide medical insurance or any of those administrative headaches. I'll show you how to hire later in this book).

The rest of the book is focused on showing you exactly how you can create a virtual wholesaling company that can be run almost on autopilot, with nearly little input from you, no matter where you are in the world – through automating and outsourcing.

Two Concerns That Newbie Real Estate Investors Always Ask

Okay, before we go on any further, I need to address a question that you're probably asking: "Hey DM, automating and outsourcing sound expensive and I don't have a lot of money right now to afford them."

I hear this from a lot of aspiring real estate investors and there have been a few who get this far in my training or mentoring and decide that the cost might be too high and they go back to their tied-to-the-desk "job" of flipping houses and not having enough hours in the day to do their work.

So let me clear the air about the "cost" of automating and outsourcing.

Everything in life requires an investment of some kind: With your job, you "invested" some of your time each day in order to get a return on your time-investment – your paycheck. If you want to put money into a 401(k), you "invest" some of the money you earned from the time you spent at work. If you've flipped a property before, you "invested" money plus time plus effort in order to get a return on your investment – more money from the sale of the property.

You with me so far? Now here is where your paradigm is going to shift: Most people invest **time** in order to get **money**. That's the case for everyone who works at a job and for any real estate investor who spends their day with their ear glued to their phone or with a hammer in their hand.

And if you trade time in order to get money, what do you end up with? Only a little bit of money and no time to spend it... and no time to make more money.

Now think about the most successful people in the world – the Richard Bransons and Donald Trumps and Robert Kiyosakis and others.

We invest **money** in order to get **time**.

And for those of us who invest money to get time, what do we end up with? More time to make more money, which is a positive cycle that eventually leaves us with a lot of money and a lot of time!

Let's look at the same concept in a different way:

Everything in your life has a value attached to it – including the time you have available in your day. Let's say (just as an example only, so you can see what I'm talking about) that your time is worth $50.00/hour. Maybe it's worth more or maybe it's worth less but let's just use this number as an example.

If you choose to do all of the work yourself in your real estate investing business, you are valuing all efforts the same – $50.00/hour – whether you're hammering nails or sweeping the dirt or mowing the lawn or answering the phone or talking to potential buyers.

And here's an added problem: You only have 16 or 18 hours of "awake" time during your day so the most you can ever earn (if you work 18 hours each and every day) is $900/day or $4500 for a 5-day week. That sounds like a decent wage but it also sounds like a recipe for burnout and never seeing your family!

But if you invest some money to automate and outsource (that's working ON your business instead of IN it), you might spend a little bit of money but your earning potential skyrockets.

Let's continue the example to illustrate: Let's say that your time is worth $50.00/hour and you hire someone to do some of your work for you. And let's say that you pay them $3.00 per hour. (I know what you're thinking: "No one will work for $3.00 an hour". Well what if I told you that you can get high-level, hard-working people for that or even less than that!?! I'll show you how later in this book).

If you get the person you hired to do one hour of work, you make $47.00 an hour because the other person is doing your work for much less than the amount of money your time is worth, plus you didn't have to work that hour!

Now let's take this even further (and this will really blow your mind!).

What if you got two people to do some work in that hour? You pay each person $3.00/hour. But they are doing twice the amount of work for you. So they are achieving two hours of your work in only one hour (that's a value of $100.00) but it's only costing you $6.00... PLUS you're not working! You're hanging out with your family or doing something else in your business.

Let's take this even one step further: Imagine how much more successful you'd be if you outsourced even one hour to those two people PLUS you spent that hour doing something that helped to build your real estate investing business – maybe do another deal or deepen your relationships with potential buyers. That's entrepreneur-leadership; that's being a business owner/investor; that's working ON your business instead of IN your business.

What an amazing concept and the potential for financial freedom and time freedom is exciting. **The best thing you can do**

for your business is to adopt the mindset of investing money to get more time by automating and outsourcing... because you value your time and can use it to get more money!

In the example I gave above, I only talked about two people doing two hours of work for you. But you can do so much more.

The rule of compounding: Compounding is when one thing builds on another and then both of those things build on a third, and so on. You might have heard of compounding interest, which basically means that your initial principal and any additional interest all earns interest.

The same is true for your business: When you spend one hour of your own time to work, you get one hour of work. But when you get other people (at a lower rate) to work that hour for you, you get a compounding benefit. Imagine how productive your business would be if you got one or two or ten people working for you!

Using the numbers I gave above, just imagine what life would be like if you stopped working for one 8-hour day and instead you hired 1 person to work your 8-hour day for you at $3.00/hour. Your day is valued at $400.00 ($50.00 x 8 hours) but you only pay $24.00 ($3.00 x 8 hours). For less than half of what *one* of your hours is worth, you get a full day of work out of this person!

Now let's push the power of compounding even further: What if you hired two people to work a full day and you paid them $3.00 an hour each? You end up paying out $48.00 (worth almost one of your hours) and you get two days' worth of work from them! For less than what you earn in one hour, you have just got two days of work done!

In virtual wholesaling you have the potential to automate and outsource almost ALL of your business to others, allowing you to earn a lot of money without putting in the effort or spending a lot of money.

The other concern people have when they learn about outsourcing and automating is the issue of control. They wonder,

"Hey DM, won't I end up having to clean up the mistakes that other people make?"

My response to this concern is that, yes, people make mistakes. However, there is very little in life that can't be undone and very few mistakes that can't be corrected. And if you hire the right people and teach them what you want them to do and then keep an eye on them, mistakes don't happen very often. I explain all of this in upcoming chapters so keep reading and I'll reveal the things you need to know!

If you're not careful, running a real estate investing business can become a time-trap that you get caught in, which keeps you from pursuing those lifestyle dreams and goals that I talked about in the first chapter.

But if you set up your real estate investing business to run virtually, you suddenly have the financial freedom and time freedom to do whatever you want.

"Who dares wins"

- Motto of the SAS

The DM's Action Steps From This Chapter

1. Calculate how much your time is worth right now. (Usually the hourly equivalent of your wage is a good starting point). Then ask yourself: Is every task you're doing in your business right now worth that hourly rate?

2. List the fears and challenges that might hold you back from making the switch to working ON your business instead of IN your business.

"Energy and persistence conquer all things."

- Benjamin Franklin

PART 2

GETTING STARTED IN VIRTUAL WHOLESALING

In Part 1 of this book I talked about aspirations and mindset. I showed you why many people weren't living the type of life they wanted to live and I revealed what held many of them back.

I also shared my belief that virtual wholesaling is the best way to create the life you want to live. And although not every person will necessarily succeed at the same level, virtual wholesaling has the potential to give you the freedom you desire.

I also talked about the mindset required to start and grow a real estate investing business. This mindset might seem strange to most people (who are used to showing up and working hard in an attempt to be successful – even though those things aren't connected). Some readers will struggle with implementing the ideas I'm presenting because they can't adopt this new mindset. But if you can adopt the mindset I've discussed, it can change your life.

In Part 2, I want to show you HOW to set up your virtual wholesaling business so that it can run without you. Now we're getting into the nuts-and-bolts of starting up your real estate investing business.

Before we go any further, I want to highlight something important: It's easy to put down the book right now and think "I would love to be a real estate investor"… and then never do anything about it. Because so far, all we've done is learn about the opportunity.

But now we're actually taking action. I'm outlining in this part of the book exactly what you need to do. So if you're tempted to put the book down at this point, DON'T!!! If so, I can guarantee that some of you will pick up this book again next year and read the first part of the book again and wish you had started investing earlier.

This is where the rubber meets the road. This part of the book tells you the actions you need to take. Many aspiring real estate investors give all kinds of reasons (excuses) why they can't get started as real estate investors and in this part of the book I'm hoping to take away all of those reasons by showing you exactly what you need to do.

"The superior [person] is modest in [their] speech, but exceeds in [their] actions."

- Confucius

CHAPTER 4

HOW TO SET UP YOUR REAL ESTATE INVESTING BUSINESS SO IT RUNS ALMOST ON ITS OWN (WHILE YOU LAY ON THE BEACH)

Venice, Italy 5:56 PM
Writing from a canal-side cafe

Just a few minutes ago, Deena and I completed a gondola ride. It was unreal to float through the canals and check out the ancient buildings that rise up out of the water – we just don't have anything like it in the U.S.

As we floated through the canals, I was reminded just how fortunate I am to do what I do. Most of the people who are considered "successful" by popular standards (i.e. doctors, lawyers) are stuck in their offices while I spend my days in these amazing places.

I can't think of any other jobs/occupations that give you the freedom to do this. Unfortunately, even real estate investors don't always have the freedom to do what they want during the day. Instead, they are stuck to their desk or they have a hammer in their hand and they spend their days working.

Years ago, I realized that the life I wanted to live was one where I got to travel – not one where I had a phone glued to my ear. So I built my real estate investing business to operate without me. Yes, I still run my business but the day-to-day is pretty much automatic.

I wanted to see the world. I wanted to float through Venice on a gondola. And I didn't want to get calls from prospective sellers or investor-buyers while I was traveling.

It is possible to build a real estate investing business like that. In this chapter, I'll show you how.

How To Create A Virtual Business – The Basics

There is a gap between what most people dream about and the way they live. They dream about having the freedom to spend time doing the things they enjoy but they spend their time in a completely opposite way – spending most of their time working long hours to achieve what they hope is freedom someday in the future. (It rarely materializes).

Close your eyes and think about the life you want to be living right now. Think about all the things you want to be doing. Chances are, your work is standing in the way of the freedom you desire.

Instead of working hard now to (hopefully) enjoy freedom in the distant future when you retire, why not build a real estate investing business that allows you to enjoy that lifestyle now? That's the power of virtual wholesaling!

Wholesaling is a familiar type of real estate investing where you put undervalued properties under contract and then you sell the contract to an investor-buyer. And **virtual** wholesaling takes it to a whole new level by operating almost automatically without a lot of input from you. Virtual wholesaling means that you can run a real estate wholesaling business virtually – without being present in an office, without being glued to the phone all day long; you can do it from anywhere.

To build a real estate investing business that runs without you, you need to build it with the right pieces in place to operate with only minimal direction from you. Using the power of outsourcing and automation, you'll create a wholesaling business that runs virtually.

The pieces to build your virtual wholesaling system are something I call the 3 T's of virtual wholesaling: **Team** and **Tools** and **Technology**.

You'll create a team of people who are on the ground, doing the work you yourself can't do or don't want to do (because you're too busy spending time with your kids or your spouse or fly-fishing at your favorite river or floating down the canals of

66

Venice in a gondola).

You'll harness the power of tools and technology to speed up communication and automate a lot of the processes that could otherwise take up hours of valuable time.

Let's look at the team and the tools/technology that you'll need and then later in the chapter I'll show you how to put all these pieces in place.

Who To Put On Your Real Estate Investing Team

The three must-have people on your team:

Virtual assistant. A key player on your virtual wholesaling team is a virtual assistant. This is one of the first people you should add to your team.

A virtual assistant is an administrative assistant who does their work out of their own home using their own computer. You communicate by them through email or phone/Skype. You never even meet them (in fact, they might not even live in the same country).

Now, I know what you're probably thinking: "Why would I need a secretary? I'm just starting out!" I hear similar questions like that whenever I talk about virtual assistants. But virtual assistants are so much more than secretaries! They can do all kinds of administrative work, detailed work, data collection, research and coordination. Don't think of them as secretaries; think of them as your own personal director of operations for your real estate business. They are highly skilled generalists who can do a variety of tasks (probably more than you initially realize)...

... and the best part is, you can hire them very cheaply!

The DM explains...
A virtual assistant might be someone in this country or in another country. In the US, there are many stay-at-home-moms who offer virtual assistance work on the side to earn a little

extra income. And in other countries (such as India and the Philippines), virtual assistants are a huge industry where professionals offer their "VA" services to business owners who need to hire some inexpensive help. But if you're concerned about whether these virtual assistants will be fluent in your language, don't worry. Many virtual assistants train hard to become fluent in American English (and not only that, the really good ones can speak American English without a foreign accent). If you didn't know that they were in another country, you wouldn't be able to guess from communicating with them via Skype or email.

As you continue in this book, you'll read about many wholesaling tasks you can delegate to them and you'll probably be surprised at just what you can take off of your plate and put onto theirs. (Remember: They're very inexpensive so use them for as much of the detail work as possible and use your own valuable time to work ON your business). And later in the book you'll read about a successful real estate investor who uses his Philippine-based virtual assistants to answer phone calls (without any expensive international long distance charges!).

You can find your own virtual assistant by going to this exclusive link (www.VirtualRealEstateMadeEasy.com/va) and posting a project for a virtual assistant. You'll get many people replying to your project and you can pick the best one for your needs.

Before we continue on, let's take a quick break as I give you some of my best ideas and tips to help you work more effectively with a virtual assistant...

The DM's Top Tips to Work with a Virtual Assistant:

1. *Show your virtual assistant the big picture.*
    Explain to them how they fit into your virtual

wholesaling business.

2. *Make your goals and tasks clear. When you explain something, be clear about what you expect. Remember, you're a leader! They will do a great job for you if you help them know how to do a great job for you.*

3. *Help your virtual assistant be as successful as they can by giving them checklists and step-by-step guides. This helps them to report to you accurately if you ever need an update and to identify areas to fix if a mistake is made.*

4. *If chosen carefully, your virtual assistant is a professional who knows what they are doing: Don't expect everything to turn out exactly the way you envision it. (Just because you picture something happening one way, doesn't mean that the virtual assistant will complete it in that way). As long as your virtual wholesaling business is progressing successfully, and everything is legal and ethical, give your virtual assistant a little latitude to do their job the way they do it best.*

5. *Don't micromanage your assistant. You are getting an assistant in order to be virtual. If you micromanage your assistant then you're not virtual.*

6. *Praise your virtual assistant generously! Remember, a simple "thank you" or "you're doing a great job" goes a long, long way. You'd be surprised!*

When you find a good virtual assistant, follow these tips to work with them more effectively. (And keep reading because later in this book you'll read about a very successful real estate investor who has more than one virtual assistant working for him full-time! It's an exciting story to read).

Lawyer. A good lawyer will not only keep your business legal and keep you from being surprised by some obscure law you didn't know about, but they will also proactively help you run a better business by making suggestions about how to build a business that maximizes the opportunities and minimizes the liabilities and risks.

You should resist the temptation to hire your lawyer friend, or the lawyer who specializes in divorce and is extremely cheap.

Find a lawyer who has experience with real estate (better yet, find someone who has real estate investing experience) so they won't waste your time researching the unusual (but legal!) deals that real estate investors do.

You can find a lawyer who is savvy about real estate investing by visiting your local real estate investing clubs and asking them for a recommendation.

I always advise that one of the best first investments you can make with a lawyer is to pay them for an hour of their time and then go in there and ask a million and one questions. You'll educate yourself, they'll learn just how serious you are about investing, and you'll know what they are talking about as you work together.

And again, find a lawyer who is able to work with you virtually, so you can be surfing the waves in Australia or climbing the Himalayas and not have to show up at their office to ask or answer a question they might have.

Mentor. A mentor is just as essential as the other members of your team. To be honest with you, you wouldn't be reading this book if I didn't have mentors in my life, You need one or more mentors – someone who has done it before and can help you do it too.

A mentor can help you figure out your strengths and weaknesses, and they can help to connect you to new opportunities and find even more success in existing opportunities.

This is key! Find a mentor you like and engage them. Invest in yourself and your future, it's so worth it! Every successful person I know has one or more mentors. (I may be The DM and mentor others but I still have mentors and always will for life... it's needed in many parts of life and business. As I write this, I have 4 mentors in different parts of my business and life.)

To find mentors, identify a few areas where you need to grow and start there. Divide up the business of wholesaling into smaller parts and figure out which parts you're not comfortable with then pick a mentor to help you focus on that specific aspect. For example, find a mentor who is familiar with virtual wholesaling and can show you how to run your business virtually. Or find a mentor who knows management and leadership skills and can help you manage your team.

When some people think of mentors, they think of meeting with them face-to-face for coffee once a month or so. But mentors can actually come in different forms. You don't always have to meet with them face-to-face. Here are some ways you can be mentored:

- Get in touch with a potential mentor and ask to email them a couple of questions each week.

- Find someone who really knows the topic that you want to be mentored in and read everything they've written on the topic – blogs, books, etc.

- Find a potential mentor and subscribe to their blog, sign up for webinars they put on, and follow everything they do online and offline.

Mentors should be a key part of your team and you should plan to always have at least one mentor that you follow closely.

And here's one more key point about mentors I need to make: A mentor isn't someone who does everything for you. They are there to give you direction so you can do something yourself. (Unfortunately, many people make this mistake and ask mentors for much more). Think of it as if you are driving in an area you're not familiar with and you get lost. You stop at a local gas station to ask for direction from a person who's lived in this area their whole life. They know all the roads inside and out and YOU are totally off track and lost. When you ask them for help, do you get them to drive your car? Of course not! You get them to give you the exact direction and you take action from there.

Before we continue, let's take a quick break and look at my best advice on how you can work more effectively with a mentor to really drink in what they have to say and benefit from it...

The DM's Top Tips to Work with a Mentor:

1. *Find mentors for specific areas of your business. Don't just find one mentor in your business. Find a few mentors.*

2. *Make sure that the mentors you choose are people you aspire to be like. If you want to be successful but you don't like a successful person's personality, it doesn't matter how successful they are, you won't learn a lot from them because you don't want to be like them. So make sure that you actually want to be like your mentor in the area you want to grow.*

3. *Know exactly what you want to get out of the relationship. For example, don't just approach a mentor and ask them – in general – to be your mentor. Instead, know the area that you'd like to make some changes in and*

let the mentor know what you've identified. Tell your mentor why you chose them.

4. *Decide if the person you want to mentor you will be someone you actually talk or email with or if you will just be "mentored" by them through their books and websites.*

5. *If you want to be mentored by someone by contacting them (i.e., via email), be sure to do some research about them first. Get to know them; read their books, visit their website, etc. That way, you won't be starting at "zero" in your relationship; you'll already have some initial knowledge.*

6. *If you are going to contact someone to be your mentor, clearly outline what you hope to achieve from the relationship and how much of their time you're asking for. For example, let them know ahead of time that you'd like to email them once a week with questions you have.*

7. *Be respectful of your mentor's time. Get in touch with them periodically but don't hassle them. Keep it within the limitations of what you set out when you approached them initially.*

8. *You might be the learner but you can still be active in the relationship. Constantly apply what you learn and ask questions. Do additional research and come back to the mentor with your thoughts and ideas.*

9. *This is key: Act on what your mentor tells you.*

A mentor who doesn't inspire you to change isn't very valuable. So if a mentor tells you something, act on it. Do what they suggest.

10. *Don't forget to thank your mentor! They are taking time to help you (time that could be spent doing other things). Show your gratitude to them with a simple thank you. And when you grow and become very successful, don't forget who help you get you there! I'm actually friends now with many of my first mentors and will continue to be friends with them as it's a rare breed of folks who implement.*

So far, I've covered the people you need to have on your team. There are two other optional team members you might also work with (but these aren't always necessary). I'll explain what these team members do and why you might choose to have some of them on your team.

Contractors. In some types of real estate investing, you work pretty closely with several contractors. But with wholesaling, you're not rehabbing a property so you won't actually be dealing with a lot of contractors.

However, it's really helpful to have a couple of contractors with whom you have a great relationship. If necessary, they can swoop in and fix a minor problem quickly or they can drive by a property and give you an idea of what kind of shape the property is in.

You won't be paying them for a lot of work, so don't worry about this as a huge expense. But their insight and quick fixes can sometimes help you out. Get to know some contractors in the area where you invest. You'll be able to hand them off to your new buyers as you grow so it's a win/win for all.

74

Real estate agents. I call this person an "optional" member of your team because I really want you to get going and not to hold back just because you don't have an agent on your team yet. But once you get going, you can add them to your team and they'll help your real estate business grow.

A good real estate agent can help you in many ways. Just to list a couple of the ways that they can help you...

1. A real estate agent can be a source of investor-buyer leads: Let the agent know what type of deal you have and they can let their investor clients know about you and your deal.

2. A real estate agent can also be a good lead for deals that you can wholesale. Ask the agent about what type of deals they have access to.

So you can use real estate agents to help you find deals and wholesale them to investor-buyers.

But note: Make sure that your real estate agent is investor-friendly. Not all agents are created equal and some agents aren't creative enough to work with investors. Some agents are just in the habit of listing a house, selling it, and collecting their standard commission. Anything outside of that "typical" scenario doesn't fit for them. But real estate investors frequently work in those situations where a real estate agent might not be helpful!

You need to find a real estate agent who is creative and investor-friendly enough to see a deal and, if they can't sell it themselves, they'll get in touch with you to let you know about it.

What Tools and Technology You Need to Automate Your Real Estate Investing Business

There are some essential tools that you absolutely need if you want to be a virtual wholesaler. Later, I'll tell you about a great piece of technology that can dramatically improve your results.

Website: When most real estate investors start out, they post their telephone number everywhere, hoping for people to call them. Guess what happens: If people call, the real estate investor has to answer. That's not a way to be a virtual real estate investor because you can't go very far from your phone just in case it rings.

Virtual real estate investors who choose to give out their number can set it up so their phone is routed to their virtual assistant. And, virtual real estate investors can also use a website, which potential sellers or investors can visit to answer questions and fill out an online form.

To build your virtual wholesaling business so that you don't have to always be near a phone, add your website address and your phone number to your marketing (and make sure that your phone number is forwarded to your virtual assistant).

(Many real estate investors will only put their phone number on their marketing and then they are stuck near the phone all day as they don't have a funnel to patch calls through to their assistant. And they neglect to put a website on at all even though the National Association of Realtors reported that 82% of all home searches begin with an online search).

What that means is: If you're not using a website, you're missing out on the majority of potential buyers.

Building a website is really easy and you'll be surprised at how affordable it is. (Years ago, websites cost thousands or even tens of thousands of dollars to build but now, great looking website can be set up for only a fraction of the price).

A great place to go for a website is VirtualRealEstateWebsites.com, which is template-based and enables you to put together a great looking website in just a few clicks – no coding needed. All you need to do is fill in couple blanks and voila, you have a website to promote to the world.

You don't need anything fancy, just a couple of pages that tell people who you are and what you do. A little later in the book I'll show you what you need to put on your website to almost entirely automate a key part of the business that used to take investors hours every day to do.

Email autoresponder: The other tool you need is an email autoresponder. (If you're not sure what this is, don't shut the book or tune me out... I'll show you what it is and why you need this).

An email autoresponder is a simple to use as email but it has some other amazing functionality, too. But as long as you know how to use email, you know how to use an email autoresponder!

You're probably already familiar with what an autoresponder is (even if you don't know what it's called) – it's when you visit a website or blog and are prompted to leave your name and email on the site. When you do, you are subscribed to that business' autoresponder and emails will drip out to you periodically (for example, once a week or once a month or every day).

Your virtual real estate business will be doing the same thing – you'll have a simple sign-up form on your website and investor-buyers will sign up and receive your emails periodically. (Don't worry; it's fast, easy, requires no technical skill, and it's something you can get your virtual assistant to do for you).

There are a couple of reasons why you want to use an email autoresponder rather than just a standard email:

- Email autoresponders automate part of the process for you that you would otherwise have to do on your own.

- Email autoresponders allow you to schedule messages to be sent later – and even schedule a series of messages to be sent later – so this part of your business can run without you while you are playing a round of golf or hanging out at the waterpark with your children or grandchildren.

- Email autoresponders are designed to help more of your emails get to the recipients. (Without getting too technical, here's the reason: Lots of email systems have spam software that might reject emails from a normal email system but allow through autoresponder emails).

That's all I'm going to say about email autoresponders because it's so much like email that it's super-easy to use but better for your business.

The DM explains...

I know many will read about autoresponders and get freaked out. I get it. I was too when I first learned about it. But after I saw how much time I save and how much money I make because of them, I'll use them forever. Plus, if you're like me and hate talking to tire kickers (people who just want to learn more but will never move forward on a deal), then this is one way to keep them from wasting your time.

It won't take long to understand how autoresponders work and once you know how to use it (remember: it's as simple as sending an email) you can communicate to dozens or even hundreds or even thousands or even tens of thousands of investor-buyers with a single email sent with the touch of a single button. If that's not working smart instead of hard, I don't know what is!

Call broadcast system. Until now, most investors would make calls one-at-a-time to potential investor-buyers, to see if they are interested in a property, and sellers to see if they are interested in selling. That takes time and it requires you to be near a phone (obviously!). And the worst part: It resulted in a lot of rejection as the investor heard one "no" after another "no" after yet another "no".

But a call broadcast system is a really simple to use tool that enables you to record one call and then it automatically calls everyone on your phone list with your message. If they're interested, they can get back to you. If they're not interested, they just hang up.

You can record the call but you don't have to be in the office when the call goes out and you never hear another "no" again!

Once you have all of these pieces in place, you have everything you need to get started as a virtual wholesaler. Throughout the rest of the book, I'm going to describe how you'll run your virtual wholesaling business so that your team does most of the work and your tools and technology automates most everything.

By putting all of these pieces in place, you are working on your business instead of working in your business. And with everything running automatically without you, you'll have the freedom you want to live the life you want to live.

One last note: Many aspiring investors are going to read this chapter then put down the book and move on to something else. Resist that temptation! Invest in your virtual wholesaling business – and your freedom! – by putting together your team and getting the tools and technology to be successful.

Then join me in the next chapter and I'll show you how to put it all together.

The DM's Action Steps From This Chapter

1. Post a project to hire a virtual assistant at www.VirtualRealEstateMadeEasy.com/va.

2. Schedule time to talk with a lawyer who knows about real estate investing.

3. Find two or three mentors who can help you with various aspects of your virtual wholesaling business.

4. Set up your virtual wholesaling website (visit www.VirtualRealEstateWebsites.com for a fast, easy way to get it all set up).

5. Set up your autoresponder tool by going to www.DiscountEmailFollowup.com and signing up. This is the same tool I use!

6. Set up the free phone broadcasting account by going to www.CallToProfits.com and signing up. This is the same tool I use!

CHAPTER 5

HOW TO BUILD RELATIONSHIPS WITH INVESTOR-BUYERS SO THEY BECOME RABID FANS WHO ACTIVELY DO DEALS WITH YOU

Malibu, California 7:30 PM
Writing from my ocean-side condo

I'm writing this from my ocean-side condo. Yeah, I realize that Malibu isn't as exotic as some of the other locations I've been to – Paris, France; Santorini, Greece; Venice Italy; etc. – but as I was sitting here listening to the surf, I was reminded that virtual wholesaling is about having the freedom to do what you want – you don't have to travel, of course. The benefit of virtual wholesaling is not necessarily that you can do it anywhere; rather, the benefit is that it is almost entirely automated so you don't have to do very much at all. Get it?

You can travel if you want – there is so much to see in the world and that is what I have chosen to do. But you don't have to.

I'm mentioning this because I occasionally hear of aspiring real estate investors who say: "I don't need to know how to do virtual wholesaling because I don't need to be virtual". Maybe they get scared off by the word "virtual" or they assume that just because you can do this virtually, you probably will.

Nothing could be further from the truth! Virtual wholesaling just means that you can run your business from anywhere (and any time) – whether you want to run it from Peru or Australia or Finland or South Africa... or from the comfort of your own home.

Virtual wholesaling is perfect for any lifestyle because it can give you the time freedom and financial freedom to spend your time doing what you want to do.

And don't get scared off by the word "virtual". It's not a high-tech business. Anyone of any age and technical ability can run a virtual wholesaling business because it is so simple to do. If you can use email, you can be a virtual wholesaler.

In a previous chapter, I gave you all of the pieces of the puzzle – the team you're going to put together and the tools/technology you need.

The list is really simple – and smaller than most people realize! But just knowing what components you need isn't going to turn you into a real estate investor. Now we need to put it all together. And it starts in a way that just might surprise you.

The Biggest Mistake Many New Real Estate Investors Make

Real estate investing is all about finding a potential deal and then matching it up with a buyer or renter. It doesn't matter what kind of real estate investing we're talking about.

And with wholesaling, it's all about finding a great deal and putting it under contract and then assigning your interest to an investor-buyer.

When most people think of wholesaling, they think of it being done in the following steps:

1. Find a property

2. Put it under contract

3. Search for investor-buyers

4. Sell the contract to them.

It seems like the simplest form of real estate investing, doesn't it? And if you were to get started without any guidance from anyone, the approach you might take would be similar to the approach that many real estate investors take:

They comb through various sources to find deals and then they get in touch with the sellers to inquire about the price and to check out the property.

Once they put the deal under contract, then it's time to find some investor-buyers who will buy the deal. The wholesaler picks up the phone and calls the first investor-buyer and says, "Hey! I've got a great deal for you, when can I show it to you?" If the investor-buyer has the time and the capital and the interest, they'll set up an appointment.

A few days later, the wholesaler presents the deal and the investor-buyer thinks about it and then declines.

So the wholesaler makes the next call…

And the next…

And the next…

And the next…

Until the wholesaler finally finds someone who is willing to invest in the deal (if they ever find them).

This might seem like the method that makes the most sense but there are some serious problems with it:

- It's time consuming! You're spending most of your time looking for deals, and once you accomplish that, now you're spending your time calling on investor-buyers!

- It's exhausting! You're faced with the negativity of hearing one "no" after another.

- It's stressful! You put the property under contract and you have a short time to sell that contract to an investor-buyer. As each day ticks by, you're left wondering if you are going to lose the deal.

- Ultimately, it's work-intensive! You don't get to enjoy the lifestyle you're dreaming of

because you're so busy presenting to one
investor-buyer after another.

This method of wholesaling is no different than having a job that you have to go to every day. It's even the method I thought I needed to do when I first started wholesaling... until I got sick of the run-around (answering phones and trying to find investor-buyers for my deals) and I wondered if there was a better way. I stumbled by accident onto the techniques that have allowed me to run a virtual real estate investing business from anywhere in the world. Now I'm sharing that better way with you.

Here's the virtual way to wholesale, using the tools and technology that I described in an earlier chapter:

It's a paradigm shift. Instead of thinking about the deal first and then trying to find someone to fill it, think of the relationship first. And the deals will almost automatically fall into place.

The Virtual Wholesaling Way

Imagine that you are wandering through the desert and you come upon a small oasis of palm trees, so you know that there is water underground. You've been wandering through the desert all day and now you're thirsty. Is that the time to start digging a well? Of course not! You're too thirsty! The best time to dig a well is *before* you are thirsty.

Although we would all agree with this idea in principle, many wholesalers do the exact opposite in their wholesaling business: They are thirsty for investor-buyers but they don't start looking for them until they already have a deal. The good news is: You can be finding deals and investor-buyers at the same time.

Instead of looking for just a deal, start by building relationships with potential investor-buyers. Dig your well of investor-buyers before you are thirsty for them. Then, when you have a great deal, you'll have a big well of investor-buyers to draw from.

84

It's a simple shift in logic but it makes perfect sense when you think of it as digging your well before you are thirsty. And you'll see in a moment just how much it can transform your wholesaling to turn it from work-intensive to virtual.

Setting everything up is really easy and can be done quickly. Once it's all set up, you're ready to go! (That's another thing I like about virtual wholesaling – it's really fast to get started and start seeing results).

So the first step to become a virtual wholesaler is to build a "deep well" of investor-buyers that you can present deals to.

Instead of building a "Rolodex" of investors that you will call, you'll use some of the tools/technology that I discussed in a previous chapter to build a relationship with them through email and phone broadcast.

With email, you can build a relationship with them by occasionally emailing them (I'll show you how) and using the tool/technology I discussed in a previous chapter, you can send out one email to all of your investors and a simple 30 second voice broadcast.

And the best part: Email is virtual! You can email from anywhere in the world (you just need access to a computer) and you can schedule emails to be sent at a certain time, so you don't even need to be at your computer when the email goes out!

Just imagine how much more effective you'll be! Rather than dialing the phone to talk to one investor-buyer with a deal (and then a second investor-buyer and then a third and then a fourth, etc.), you can send out one single email in less than two minutes – and it doesn't matter if you send it to ten or a hundred or a thousand or a hundred thousand investor-buyers. It takes just a moment and you can use these emails to build a relationship and to tell them about deals.

It also helps to cut down on the amount of rejection you'll get, too. Although you'll still hear "no" from time to time (of course), sending out emails is a way for you to tell investor-buyers about deals so that usually the most interested people respond. So you'll still hear "no" from people when you tell them about a deal but using email helps you to get only the most interested investor-buyers "raising their hand" to indicate that they're interested in learning more.

The DM explains...

Novice investors will often hear this concept and say "wow, that makes a lot of sense" but then they'll go back to the conventional (time-consuming) way of real estate investing because it's familiar and it seems like you're busier (but that's because you're working in your business instead of on your business). Take some time to wrap your mind around this method of "digging your well before you are thirsty" and it will transform how successful your real estate investing business will become!

Imagine how much time that will save you! Before, you might have had to telephone a dozen (or more) potential investors just to get a couple of meetings and maybe you'd close the deal from one of those meetings. That is hours and hours of work. But with email, you fire out an email about a deal and the interested investor-buyers will respond for more information.

So, how do you build a relationship via email?

How To Build A Relationship With Your Potential Investor-Buyers

When most new real estate investors first hear about the system I'm describing, they can have a hard time wrapping their minds around the possibility of building a relationship with investor-buyers through email. But it is possible! I'll show you how but first you need to know how to set it up correctly.

The first thing you want to do is set up a system so you can capture email addresses of interested investor-buyers and then email that growing list.

To make it easy and effective and totally automated, you'll need a website and your email autoresponder.

Websites used to be a really complicated and expensive step but it has become very easy and affordable lately. Your website doesn't have to be very detailed, it just needs to tell people about who you are and it will show them that you are a serious investor.

There are lots of website-building tools that can help (and again, your virtual assistant will be able to help you, too). As I mentioned in an earlier chapter, a site like VirtualRealEstateWebsites.com is a great tool to use (and I use it).

You only really need a one-page website that briefly tells potential investor-buyers about you. This is known as a squeeze page. You may think you need a big website with lots of pages and content (and it's okay to have a big site with plenty of content) but the main goal is to get the prospect to leave their name and email address so you can start building trust with them. A percentage of website visitors will do this if your message is congruent with what they want and if they think you might be able to help them.

Then, simply add an email sign-up form on your website (and if you use VirtualRealEstateWebsites.com then this is all built in, by the way).

That's all you need to get started. People will come to your website (I'll show you how to get them there) and they'll leave their email address and then they are added to your list of investor-buyers automatically… and suddenly you've dug a well before you're thirsty. It's really that easy.

Here's a bonus tip for you: If you want to increase the likelihood that people give their email address, you can offer a free report in exchange for their email address.

Have your virtual assistant write up a report and add it to your email autoresponder tool. On your website, tell them that they'll get a free report for leaving their email address.

Some report topics might include:

- Ways to become a real estate investor

- Tips to increasing success as a real estate investor

- Things to watch out for when investing in real estate

- How to increase property value by doing a simple fix-up

- How to get access to capital using self-directed IRA's

If you use VirtualRealEstateWebsites.com, you'll get these reports for free as well.

In an upcoming chapter, I'll tell you how to do virtual marketing so that eager investor-buyers want to visit your website and sign up, without you having to do any work at all. But now I want to talk about how to build a relationship with investor-buyers through email.

When aspiring virtual wholesalers hear about this, they wonder: "How can I possibly build a relationship with hundreds or even thousands of investor-buyers via email?" Keep reading; I'll show you how!

All relationships develop over time as two people build trust and learn about each other. That's true of every relationship whether it's a friendly relationship, a romantic relationship, or (as in our case) a business relationship.

In a budding romantic relationship, for example, you don't ask to marry the other person when you're on the first date! The first date is just to get to know them and see if you are each interested in spending a little more time together.

As a first date leads to a second date and then to a third date, you spend time learning about the other person and building up trust.

Later, once you know each other and trust each other, then it's time to think about marriage.

A similar thing happens with friendship – two people might learn more about each other and discover that they have a lot in common. So they spend more time together and, in time, they discover that they are best friends.

With the exception of the schoolyard, there isn't a formal "let's be best friends!" announcement early in the relationship. It just happens as you build up trust and learn about each other.

The exact same thing happens when you're building a good relationship with investor-buyers. Too many real estate investors meet an investor-buyer and try to spring a deal on them right away, without building trust and establishing rapport. (It isn't the end of the world if you do that but it's not productive if you want to get a lot of deals done!)

So your email tool is a way for each of you (the potential investor-buyer and you) to build trust with each other.

Then, presenting a deal becomes so much easier.

Developing trust and building a relationship via email is not only possible, it's easy

In this section, I'm going to show you how it's possible to build a relationship with investor-buyers through email, regardless of whether you have one or ten or one hundred or one thousand investor-buyers on your list.

All you do is email them periodically (as I've already explained) and share a little about yourself in each email. Tell them about who you are and why you're investing, and what your background is. Share your likes and dislikes and interests and goals and even your quirks.

Of course, don't just dump everything on them all at once. Instead, regularly email them with updates about you.

And here's the most important part: Remember that all relationships are two-way streets. Don't just broadcast dry facts about yourself. Ask questions in your email. Invite your investor-buyers to reply to your email with answers.

Here's a list of things to talk about to get your brain started. In emails to your investor-buyers, share some of these facts and invite them to reply with their own information:

- Why you started wholesaling

- Your family kids, dogs, grandparents etc.

- Your professional background

- Any accomplishments or things you are great at; let them know about your achievements!

- What special skills or experience you have, especially if it helps your wholesaling

- Your hobbies – boating skiing, fishing, traveling, toy trains etc.

- Your favorite vacation – talk about the time you were on vacation and you were so relaxed, etc.

- Where you grew up as a child (it's good to share things like this).

- Share with them your Facebook page so they can see pictures and learn more about you. (Make sure to be professional on your Facebook page but keep your personality intact).

Not everyone will reply. That's okay. But by you sharing with them and inviting them to reply, they'll feel like they know and trust you (even if they don't respond to every email); and, you'll build up a pretty good knowledge of your investor-buyers, especially the ones who most actively respond to you.

Let's pause for a moment to review some of my top tips to help you build a relationship with your investor-buyers...

The DM's Top Tips to Building a Relationship With Your Investor-Buyers via Email:

- *Don't dump everything on them all at once. Share a bit at a time.*

- *Keep it light. Share a bit about yourself with them but stay positive. Avoid some of those darker and more challenging moments in life.*

- *Invite them to respond with similar information to you.*

- *Don't make every email a revelation about yourself. Email your list of investor-buyers occasionally (weekly is good) and sometimes tell them about yourself and sometimes tell them about a deal and sometimes add value with information that they might find helpful.*

- *When they reply, send them a personal email thanking them for sharing. Ask them a further question or two about themselves, just as you would with any other face-to-face conversation.*

- *Be yourself! Don't try to be someone you're not. People can spot a fake. Be genuine and you'll build a surprisingly deep relationship with your buyers.*

Those are some of my best ideas for building relationships with your investor-buyers. Just remember: Building relationships via email is no different than building relationships face-to-face or over the phone. It's all about sharing and learning and developing that foundation of trust.

Before long, your investor-buyers will feel like they know you, and you'll feel like you know many of them! And when a deal does come along (keep reading because I'll show you how to find them virtually), you'll have a deep well of investor-buyers who trust you and are willing to listen to you.

And the best part? You end up with a huge (and growing!) list of investor-buyers and it's almost entirely automated. They join your list through the email sign-up (there's nothing for you to do once it's set up) and your relationship-building emails take just a couple of minutes every week and you can write and send them regardless of whether you're enjoying a glass of wine in the sunshine on your back deck or you're sailing a yacht around the Mediterranean or sitting in a restaurant on vacation in the Caribbean or hanging out at Disneyland with your grandchildren.

The DM's Action Steps From This Chapter

1. Have you signed up for an autoresponder yet? If not, go do that now. Go to www.DiscountEmailFollowup.com and sign up.

2. List of some of the topics you will talk about with your investor-buyers. Remember to include topics where you share a little information about you with investor-buyers.

3. Write some of the autoresponder messages you'll send to your list of investor-buyers. Here's a link to 7 autoresponders you can customize and use for yourself! It's a $495 value and it's my gift to help you get started: www.VirtualRealEstateMadeEasy/mygifttoyou

"We are face to face with our destiny and we must meet it with high and resolute courage. For us is the life of action... Let us live in the harness, striving mightily; let us rather run the risk of wearing out than rusting out."

- Theodore Roosevelt

CHAPTER 6

HOW TO ATTRACT INVESTOR-BUYERS AND DEALS WITHOUT HEADACHES AND HASSLES (OR EVEN LIFTING A FINGER)

Paris, France 12:30 PM
Writing from a small café where we're eating lunch

I'm sitting in this café, eating lunch with Deena. We're having bread and cheese and wine – a classic European meal.

Want to know my favorite part about this meal? It's the middle of the day and instead of eating a sandwich from a lunchbox before I get back to my job, I'm in a different continent, with my fiancé, on one stop in a trip around the world.

I could have been working. If I had bought into the world's idea of success (show up and work hard, get a good education so you can get a good job), I'd be in an office somewhere. And even when I tried to break free of the paradigm by real estate investing, my early rehabbing efforts were still time-intensive and no better than a job.

Finally, thanks to many sleepless nights and some good mentors and even a near bankruptcy, I knew I needed to make a change.

So I did. And now, I'm eating in a Parisian café with my fiancé on one stop in a trip around the world. It's awesome!

But what amazes me is this: Whenever I talk to people about what I do, they say: "That sounds great but I couldn't do that" or "I wouldn't know how".

But it's so easy that I almost don't believe it myself and I'm living it! In this book, I'm sharing with you how I run a virtual wholesaling business and how you can too.

In a previous chapter I outlined the team and tools and technology you need to so you can run a wholesaling business from anywhere. And, I showed you how to put some of it together so you can build a list of investor-buyers who you can build a relationship with and present your deals to.

Once you have that put together (it's fast, by the way; it only takes a couple of hours) you're ready to flip the switch and start marketing your wholesaling business.

But don't make the mistake of skipping this chapter and running out to start putting up signs or taking out ads in newspapers. Although those can be part of the system, remember that the ultimate goal here is not just to become a wholesaler but to become a virtual wholesaler. In this chapter, I'm going to show you how you can market your wholesaling business without actually being there.

I've built my wholesaling business so that it attracts investor-buyers and deals without requiring me to sit in the office answering the telephone. That's how you should set up your business, too.

If you are out there marketing your business yourself then you are working in your business not on your business. Instead, follow what I'm about to show you in this chapter so your marketing runs on autopilot, giving you the time-freedom to work on your business and to do other things as well.

There are two kinds of marketing that I'm going to talk about. The first kind of marketing is done to attract investor-buyers to your website so they give you their email address and you can build a relationship with them. The second kind of marketing is done to find deals – potential underpriced properties you can put under contract.

Marketing To Attract Investor-Buyers

By attracting investor-buyers to send you their email, you are "digging your well before you are thirsty". It's critical to build this list first – and to continue to build this list for as long as you are a wholesaler – because the bigger the list, the more opportunities you create for yourself.

To attract investor-buyers to you, you're going to use something called a "ghost ad" or "leader ad". This is a powerful marketing tool that many businesses use (although few consumers really know about it). The ad offers an attractive deal to potential investor-buyers. But it doesn't have to be a real deal. It just needs to be a typical deal – the kind that you would offer if you have a deal.

The DM explains...
Does the idea of a "ghost ad" or "leader ad" sound strange to you? Many businesses use ghost ads to attract buyers. These ads offer one deal, which might or might not still be available by the time the buyer gets there. Ghost ads pull in potential buyers who often end up buying something else.

As you start up your real estate investing business, you'll be able to start using ads for real properties you have under contract eventually, but it's not necessary that they be properties you have under contract. You just need to attract the attention of potential investor-buyers, and you can do that with a ghost ad or leader ad first.

To market to investor-buyers virtually, all you need to do is simply give the details to your virtual assistant who can take care of it for you. And depending on where the ad goes (I'll tell you more about that in a minute), they can just configure the details to fit. Total time required for you? Just a couple of minutes to think about what information your ad needs and then to email it to your assistant – something that can be done from anywhere!

Your ad needs to do the following things (but again, it doesn't matter what your ad looks like; these details can be reconfigured quickly by your virtual assistant depending on where the ad is going to be placed):

1. It needs to capture the attention of potential investor-buyers. (If there are other real estate ads in the same place that they are viewing your ad, your ad needs to stand out. I'll explain how in a moment.)

2. It needs to whet their appetite by telling them a little about a deal and enticing them to learn more.

3. It needs to tell the investor-buyer to go to your website to learn more. (Once at your site, they'll sign up!)

Let's look at these in a little more detail:

Capture their attention. Capturing the attention of potential investor-buyers in your ads is easy. You just need to think about what investor-buyers are looking for when they invest.

Most real estate ads are pretty standard (and frankly, they're a little boring). If they have a picture, they'll show a nice picture of the house, maybe with a family smiling in front of the photo and then the details of the house – the price and how many bedrooms and where the house is located in relation to key locations.

But is an investor-buyer interested in that? No. That information is more for homebuyers who will be homeowners. Sophisticated investor-buyers want to know one thing: "How much will the return on my investment be?"

So when you are developing information for your ads,

remember what is important to your investor-buyer.

Let me give you an example: Most real estate ads will say something like: "Beautiful Upscale Home" or "Classic Home With All the Right Features" or something like that. Those headlines might catch the attention of a potential homeowner but not the attention of a potential investor-buyer.

Instead, use a headline like: "ROI: 15%" or "Cashflow of $1,200 per month". Those headlines might not appeal to potential homeowners but who cares! That's not who you want looking at your ads anyway. Those headlines appeal to investor-buyers who will be attracted to the ad and will be drawn in to learn more.

Keep reading. In a moment, I'll give you some examples of great ads that use these kinds of headlines and I'll explain a concept called "greed glands".

Whet their appetite. Once you've captured the attention of your investor-buyers with an appetite-whetting headline, you can add in more information (depending on where your virtual assistant is placing the ad – some marketing channels allow more information and some allow less).

Get potential investor-buyers interested by telling them a little more about the deal. Just remember to provide information that is relevant to them. So things like "beautifully appointed home with hardwood floors throughout" won't get investor buyers as interested as "low maintenance property with long-term tenant in place" or "no rehab work necessary" or "property values in this neighborhood have doubled in the past 2 years". See how those details could really get an investor-buyer excited?

Call to action. Once you've captured the attention of the potential investor-buyer and you've whet their appetite with more information that will really get them interested in the deal, tell them what to do.

Most real estate investors will stick their phone number at the bottom of the ad and then wait for someone to call. But that's a curse to any real estate investor because it means that you're stuck by your phone all day every day on the chance that someone will call. (And you can't take every call: If you're on another call or at your kid's piano recital you might miss a potential investor-buyer calling). That's what virtual wholesaling solves.

Instead of putting only your phone number on the bottom of the ad, put your website address with the words: "Visit www.[your-website-address].com to learn more or call and leave a message to get back to you at 555-555-5555. Give the person two ways to contact you. However, the goal is to direct them online (and ultimately, the goal is to keep you from having to answer the phone every time it rings)

Then, investor-buyers click to your website, sign up for your email, get the free bonus downloadable report and you build up your relationship with them.

When they email about the deal, you can either tell them more about the deal (if the deal hasn't already been snapped up by another one of your investor-buyers) or you can invite them to stay in touch to get access to more deals.

For example, if you don't have the deal anymore, you might say to them: "That deal is already gone but I always have more deals so I'll let you know when I have another one. In the meantime, let me know what types of deals you are looking for so I can let you know when I find a deal like that."

Your investor-buyer might tell you something like: "I'm looking for a 3 bedroom/2 bathroom bungalow in Illinois" or "I'm looking for triplexes in the Denver area", and so on. The great thing about doing that is: Your investor-buyers tell you exactly what they are looking for! Therefore, you don't have to hunt for deals and hope someone likes it enough to invest! Instead, you can go out and look for the kind of deals that your investor-buyers are specifically looking for!

I've just given you the three must-have elements that need to be in the ads your virtual assistant will implement to attract investor-buyers. These details can be moved around and added to pictures or put in text-only format, depending on where the ad is placed. But as long as every ad you put out has these three elements, you can build a list of investor-buyers and dig your well before you are thirsty.

100

Now let's talk about where to put your ads. There are several places that my virtual assistants have used in the past and use still today. I like using:

- Craigslist.com and backpage.com

- Local newspapers (such as the real estate classifieds section)

- Bandit signs – old school but still good

These are very effective ways to market for investor-buyers, most importantly because they are hands-off – your virtual assistant can implement them for you and manage the deployment of them for you.

There are many other ways to build a list of buyers – you can use forums and social media and even old-fashioned signs on community bulletin boards. But don't get too fancy when you're starting out. Use the ways I've mentioned above – use them over and over and that's all you really need to grow your list of investor-buyers right from the beginning. Make it a goal not to deter from this process until you have 200 investor-buyers on your email database.

Bonus idea: Contact real estate agents and let them know that you have "pocket" deals available. This is a real estate agent term that simply means that you are not going to list your deals, but if the agent has an investor-buyer and the investor-buyer for whatever reason can't buy a deal conventionally from them, the real estate agent simply calls you and sees if you have anything available. If you do, they will make a 3% or so commission (or, ideally, pay them 4% as it's higher than the normal commission but it will definitely get their attention). This is what I call "Loverage". Show the real estate agent some love, and they will bring you buyers frequently. Since you and I are "Leveraging" their marketing dollars and their time for FREE, that's why I call this strategy "Loverage".

Examples of ads for investor-buyers: Here are three examples of ads that you can use for investor-buyers.

I've given you only the text, which you can customize and use in classified ads (online or in the newspaper), but you can also have your virtual assistant design a nice flyer that you can use in other ways.

Advertisement
INVESTORS STEAL THIS HOME!
17% off this 4 bedroom/3.5 bathroom home – nearly 4000 square feet! Not only will you get a great deal on this home, I'll show you how you can get access to the best funding available on this home that you can acquire for less than 1% down! If this house isn't for you, no problem! We have access to many amazing deals! Click to www.website.com to find out how you can steal this home!

Advertisement
Own $100K house for $3,000
Call me/email me/go to www.website.com to get the rest of the details.

Advertisement
Duplex generates you up to 43% ROI in year 1. Call now! Or go to www.website.com to get your free ROI Report.

Do you notice something about these ads? They're short, catchy, and most importantly, they get an investor-buyer's greed glands going.

The DM explains...

When I talk about "greed glands" I mean that everyone is motivated to some degree by money or by the things it can buy. When real estate investors market properties, they often make the mistake of marketing the details of the property itself ("3 bedrooms" or "nice neighborhood") but real estate investors aren't necessarily motivated by those things. Their "greed glands" drive them to get excited about other things – huge discounts on houses, availability of funding, great return on investment (ROI), tenants are already living there, etc. When you create ads for investor-buyers, be sure to highlight the things that get an investor-buyer's greed glands going.

Your ads don't have to be long or very fancy. They just need to capture attention with the right concepts (the "greed gland" concepts) and then the investor-buyer will be motivated to take action and get in touch with you.

Marketing To Find Deals

To start this section, I just want to say this to you before proceeding: Once you really understand this business and get into it, you'll realize that there are so many deals available to you as an investor. In the beginning, you may be thinking that there aren't many deals but rest assured, you're about to see how to uncover them quickly and consistently.

As you build up your list of investor-buyers, the next thing you'll need to do is, of course, present them with deals... Which means you'll need some deals to present to your investor-buyers!

A "regular" wholesaler might comb through various sources searching for properties that they can put under contract. However, as a virtual wholesaler, you're too busy traveling the world or spending time with your kids or relaxing on the beach to search for properties yourself.

Instead, the virtual wholesaler does more strategic marketing to attract deals.

Just like the marketing you did to find investor-buyers, you'll create the details that you give to your virtual assistant and have your assistant deploy advertisements that get sellers contacting you.

Your ad needs to do the following things:

1. It needs to capture the attention of potential sellers.

2. It needs to whet their appetite by telling them a little about why they should contact you via email, website or phone.

3. It needs to tell the seller to contact you for more information. (Call to action)

Let's look at these in a little more detail:

Capture their attention. Remember how your ad for investor-buyers was written to attract their attention by highlighting something that would be of interest to them? The same holds true for marketing to potential sellers.

Think about what interests potential sellers and create attractive headlines for them. They might be interested, for example in "Fast close" or "Cash for your home".

There are two ways to market to sellers – pull marketing or push marketing.

104

- Pull marketing is when you use advertising to "pull" sellers to contact you. For example, you might use bandit signs or an advertisement at craigslist (or some other website) offering to buy homes for cash. It's called pull marketing because a seller sees the marketing and it pulls them to get in touch with you.

- Push marketing is when you actively go out and get in touch with sellers to "push" them to do a deal with you. This might include calling them or emailing them (if they posted their contact information on a classified ad, for example). I need to note that it's called "push" marketing because you are getting in touch with them to give them a little "push" to do the deal with you. It does NOT mean that you have to be pushy. Don't confuse those two uses of the word.

As you build up your list of investor-buyers, you'll want to use all available marketing techniques (both push and pull marketing) to get more deals.

Whet their appetite. Give them a little more detail about what you offer. If you work with people who are facing foreclosure, you might get them excited by "stop the dreaded bank calls today".

Again, think about what would get them excited to take action and get in touch with you.

Call to action. Lastly, your ad needs a call to action – something for them to do. The action should be clear and easy for them to act on immediately. Here are the calls to action that I use (and how to make the virtual):

- Provide a phone number that your virtual assistant will answer

- Provide an email address that your virtual assistant will respond to

- Provide a web address with a form they can fill out (which goes to your virtual assistant's inbox).

Give your virtual assistant the details that you want in your ads and have them post them at sites like Craigslist or in local newspapers.

Bandit signs also work well. You can hire someone to put up the signs in neighborhoods that you are interested in doing deals in. Remember: Think as a virtual business here! You can be sitting in Malibu, California doing deals in Columbus, Ohio... You're virtual now!

Bonus tip: Bird dogs are aspiring investors who are trying to build up some experience in the industry by bringing deals to experienced investors like you in exchange for a small finder's fee when the deal closes.

Find bird dogs and tell them what you are looking for. The more bird dogs you train, the more of an "army" of people you have looking for deals for you.

Check out www.VirtualBirdDog.com for great resources about how to build your birddog business.

Tips To Make Your Marketing More Powerful

Don't get fancy at first. Find a few solid places to market (I've listed a few in the chapter) and market there. Later, as you grow your wholesaling business, you can try new advertising places but you'll probably find a few of the channels I've mentioned will be your "bread and butter".

The secret to successful marketing is "**relentless consistency**". Find some good places and market there over and over and over and over again.

By comparison, many brand new investors will market once in a whole bunch of different places. But this makes them a mile wide and an inch deep and it's not easy to manage all those ads. Keep it simple for yourself by assigning a couple of great marketing channels to your assistant and giving them the details.

Lastly, remember to keep it virtual! Resist the temptation to do your own marketing. It might seem like fun, creative work but you don't need to do it. That's the job of your virtual assistant. Your job is to come up with the attention-getting, appetite-whetting ideas and email them to your assistant. And then you manage the numbers.

"Too many people dream of a better life but don't act; held back by fear of risk and failure. I'd rather have made a few mistakes and endured a few failures than to never have tried at all."

- The DM

The DM's Action Steps From This Chapter

1. Create 2-3 ads that you'll use to find investor-buyers.

2. Create 2-3 ads that you'll use to find deals.

3. Post those ads and get started!

"Just take action. It doesn't have to be perfect. Get it out there and fix it later. Nothing is permanent, so the most important thing is pushing forward."

- The DM

CHAPTER 7

HOW TO FIND DEALS, EVALUATE THEM, AND GET THEM UNDER CONTRACT

New Delhi, India 9:21 PM (I think!)
Writing from my room

India is unreal! I've been to a lot of countries and each one has been unique... but India is dramatically different! The sights and sounds and smells; the colors, the animals, the food, the heat. It's almost a shock if you're not prepared for how different it is.

And while I toured around (and even rode on the back of an elephant) I was doing deals. How is it possible to do a deal from the back of an elephant? It is possible and in this chapter I'm going to show you how.

For me, it hit home again just how exciting the virtual wholesaling opportunity really is. Here I am, on the other side of the world in a country that couldn't be more different than the one I'm from, and I was riding on an elephant while making deals happen.

Because of the way I had built my business, I could do deals anywhere – including from the back of an elephant.

Solving One Of The Biggest Frustrations In Real Estate Investing

So far, I've showed you how to set up your virtual wholesaling business so it can run almost on autopilot no matter where you are.

And when I describe the steps of autoresponders and virtual marketing to aspiring investors, they can see how those things could be done virtually.

But I think one of the aspects of virtual wholesaling that most people have trouble wrapping their heads around is the idea of finding deals, analyzing them, and getting them under contract.

In every other type of real estate investing, investors are driving around town, visiting the property, and often talking face-to-face with the seller to convince them to sell.

The idea of finding and analyzing deals and putting properties under contract while you're on the back of an elephant (or anywhere else) is sometimes more than some aspiring investors can fathom.

But I'll show you exactly what I do.

The most important thing to do is follow the easy steps I'm about to lay out for you. What you're going to do is develop a system that enables your virtual assistant to do most of the work for you.

Yes, it is possible to hand off most of this to your virtual assistant or bird dogs, as we mentioned in the last chapter! Because you're working on your business instead of in your business, what you're going to learn about in this chapter is creating a way for your virtual assistant to sort through all the details, narrow down the deals for you, do the research, and only send you the absolute best possible deals. It's fast and hands-off – perfect for when you're on the back of an elephant or on the back nine at your favorite golf course or at the back of the line at a ride in Disney World.

To set up your system, you need to give your virtual assistant the information they need to sort through the deals that are going to come in. By doing some basic sorting, and then basic research, you'll have enough information for you to make the final decision on any property you want to wholesale. And when we say hand off to an assistant you may be thinking, "Well I don't have one yet well!" Don't worry, if you want to do this yourself you're more than welcome to. But I'll tell you how it can be done with a virtual assistant so that you know how you can run your real estate business entirely virtual. The choice to do so, though, is obviously up to you.

Establish Criteria To Sort Through Deals

The first thing you need to decide is what kind of deals you want to do. By establishing criteria, you'll help to sort out all the deals that come to you and decide which ones you want to pursue. (And, as you'll see in a moment, developing criteria has an additional value in that it allows you to outsource some of the initial sorting).

When most new wholesalers get started, the first thing they do is create criteria about the property, including the criteria that the property has to be near them. That way, they can drive around the neighborhood and meet the sellers. But with virtual wholesaling you can do deals no matter where you are in the world so my suggestion is to decide right now that any criteria you have will not include geographic location. Be willing to look at any deal in the US. There might be other reasons not to do a deal but don't let geography stand in your way.

Your early criteria might include:

- The property needs to be a residential property (i.e. not a commercial one)

- The property needs to be a bungalow, townhouse, or multi-family property (i.e. not a condo)

- The property needs to be habitable with little or no work (i.e. not condemned)

These are just some ideas. Over time, you will develop your own list of criteria based on what your investor-buyers are looking for. As you get to know your investor-buyers, you might discover that they are really interested in properties in the Midwest or properties that need some fixing up or properties with two bathroom and three bedrooms or properties that are duplexes or properties where there is already a tenant living there – the list goes on and on.

Don't make a big list of criteria to start with because that will limit how many deals you do (and right now, the last thing you want to do is limit your deals). Keep your criteria list as small as possible and let your investor-buyers slowly influence it over time (since they will be the ones who ultimately buy your deals anyway).

Give this list of criteria to your virtual assistant (and bird dogs) and have them use it to do an initial sort of all the deal opportunities that come in via telephone or email. In just a couple of seconds, they should be able to separate out all of the properties that match your list of criteria from all of the properties that don't.

Bonus tip: You will get properties that don't match what you do. It happens. So start developing relationships with real estate investors who are interested in those types of deals and send the deal to them for a finder's fee.

For example, if you don't wholesale commercial properties, but you know a real estate investor who does, build a relationship with that investor and do a joint venture deal and/or put a deal together with the other investor with the full intention of assigning your position for a fee.

Once your virtual assistant has sorted out the properties according to your criteria, and has a shortlist of properties to take a closer look at, then it's time to...

Research Deals Virtually

Once your virtual assistant has created a shortlist of properties to take a closer look at, then it's time to dig deeper. Fortunately, that doesn't mean you have to quit playing with your kids or grandkids or come in from sitting on the beach. In fact, you don't have to do anything at all! This is something that your virtual assistant can take care of for you.

Have your virtual assistant do the following research on each property. (Note: You don't have to do very much research. You're only doing some preliminary research so you can decide if this is the right deal for your investor-buyers and so you can knowledgeably present it to them. This research is not the "be-all and end-all" of due diligence!)

- Get the ball rolling with Zillow.com and Trulia.com to get approximate home prices and rental rates of similar homes in the area. This is like a "thumbnail market comp". It's a quick and easy version of what real estate investors do when they are looking to price a house. This will give you a general idea of what similar houses in the area are selling for and renting for.

- Find out the local tax value. If the seller doesn't have the information, it's available from the local municipal office and can probably be found on the town or city's website.

- Find out if the seller is open to terms (such as seller financing, etc.), which can increase the number of investor-buyers who are interested in the property. (This is an important note so re-read this one!)

- Find out how much the seller wants to sell for.

- Find out how fast the seller wants to close.

You'll do some due diligence to see if it's a property that an investor-buyer might be interested in, and whether or not you can make some money by wholesaling the deal to an investor-buyer. And most of that due diligence work can be done by a virtual assistant.

Your assistant will pull together the important numbers into a quick Deal At-A-Glance chart and send them to you to look at. At your convenience, you can quickly review the deals and select the ones you want your virtual assistant to follow up on. I've put a blank Deal-At-A-Glance chart in the Appendix but I've also included one on the next page that is all filled out for you to review (with some helpful notes and tips).

Your assistant won't fill out all of the information on this Deal-At-A-Glance chart right away. They'll fill out some of it and more will be filled in as the deal moves forward.

As you can see by looking at the Deal-At-A-Glance chart on the following pages, this form will become a helpful reference document you'll use throughout the deal.

DEAL-AT-A-GLANCE
(Example chart with my explanations in *italics*)

Property Address: 123 Main Street

Purchase Price: $65,000 [*This is the amount you will buy the property for*]

Rehab Cost #1: $10,000 [*Put the reason in here, too, such as: Interior repairs and water damage*]

Rehab Cost #2: $5,000 - new roof

Total Money In Deal: [*Fill this in if you paid $1.00 or $10.00 to make the contract a legal contract, or if you are doing some other kind of deal and paid some additional money into the deal*]

Conservative Value: [*This is the property value*]

Bedrooms: 3

Bathrooms: 2

Square Footage: 1,100

Schedule Closing Date: September 5th

Schedule Completion Date: September 10th

Lock Box Code: 1234

Closing Attorneys: John Smith

Closing Attorneys Address: 123 Center Street

Closing Attorneys Telephone: 555-5555

Fax: 555-5556

Closing Attorneys email: email@johnsmithattorney.com

Closing Attorneys website: johnsmithattorney.com

Potential Sale Price: [*This is the amount that you will tell your investor-buyers that they can buy the property for. Think of it like this: The price you negotiated with the seller PLUS your fee to assign the contract*]

Potential Profit: $10,000

Copy in Back Office and Keep Hard Copy (If Applicable)
[*Check these off as you get them*]

Deed?
Title Insurance?
Purchase HUD?

After Purchase of Property

[*This section below is for your investor buyers. You can leave this section blank and when you hand off this Deal-at-a-Glance form to your investor-buyers, they can fill this part out.*]
Potential Sale Price:

Potential Profit:

If just wholesaling:
> **$ Before Rehab**:
> **$ After Rehab**:

After Rehab/Rent Out?

Electricity ON/OFF?

If On, Who?
If Off, Who?

Mowed Lawn Needed?

Any additional Lawn Maintenance needed?
If yes, list:

Sale of Property

Executed Contract Received?

Contract sent to Attorneys office with projected Closing Date?

Contractors aware of Closing?

Closing Attorneys:

Closing Attorneys Address:

Closing Attorneys Telephone:

Fax:

Closing Attorneys email:

Closing Attorneys website:

Closing Attorney has copy of the following:

Deed?

Title Insurance?

Purchase HUD?

ID?

LLC Papers?

POA? (If Applicable)

Wire Instructions?

Buyers Name:

Buyers Address:

Buyers Telephone:

Fax:

Email:

Out of Pocket Expenses:

Postage:

Gifts to your seller and buyer

Wire Fees:

How To Get In Touch With The Seller

Once your virtual assistant has started filling out the Deal-At-A-Glance chart and you've selected the deals you want to do, and, then you can get in touch with the seller to negotiate the purchase price. (Remember, you're not actually going to buy the property yourself. You're just negotiating to get a great deal that you will then present to investor-buyers).

Here is some of my best advice on negotiating with the seller...

The DM's Tips on Negotiating with the seller

1. *I always tell my students not to name the price first. Hear what the seller wants and negotiate from there.*

2. *Establish an absolute "ceiling" price that you don't want to pay a penny more for the property. Then offer a much lower amount. In the negotiation, expect to give a little but don't go over your price.*

3. *Before your call, get prepared! Know how much other comparable properties are going for, know how much the repairs will cost, etc. That way, you can tell the seller exactly why you arrived at your offer price. It's hard for a seller to ask for more when you show up to the conversation armed with a long list of reasons why you are offering a certain amount for their property.*

4. *Remember that the seller is emotionally involved in his or her property and will almost always want to get more money out of the property than it is worth. It's easy for brand new investors to become swayed by this emotion and relent a little, perhaps even allowing*

---

the selling price to climb higher than they intended because the seller has fond memories of the house.

5. *Never just agree to a higher price if the seller asks. Remember that a negotiation has some give-and-take. If the seller asks for a higher price, ask for something in return, like maybe terms or longer to close.*

6. *Remember that even though you do want to profit from this transaction, the seller will only agree if they also "win" in the transaction, too. So negotiate for a low price but be fair and work with the seller to understand what their key motivators are. (Hint: It's not always about the money).*

I love negotiating! It's all part of what makes me "The Deal Maker" ("The DM"). Negotiating is a skill that will help you in your real estate wholesaling business and it's well worth the time to learn to do it skillfully.

When you agree on a price with the seller, you fill out a Letter of Intent (LOI), which is a simple form that helps you gauge how serious the seller is. It outlines your intent to buy the property, as well as a target selling price. It gives you the authority to market the property as it gives you a position on the deal.

First, it gauges the seller's interest in selling their property. Some sellers think they want to sell their property but when it comes time to get real and sign their name on a document, the reality hits and they can't do it. They're still in the thinking-about-it stage and may choose never to sell. So the LOI is a great way for you to see how interested they are in selling. If they sign the form, they're motivated. If they won't sign the form, they're not motivated yet.

Second, the Letter of Intent gives you the right but not the obligation to purchase the property. It puts the property under your control without requiring you to spend any money.

Once you have the Letter of Intent in hand, you have the time to do any additional due diligence you need to do. Once you're happy with the property and ready to move forward, then you can go back to them to get them to sign an Option to Purchase the property.

On the next page, I've included an example of a Letter of Intent filled out (with notes and tips) for you to review and you can find a blank copy in the Appendix at the back of this book.

Letter Of Intent
(Example LOI with my explanations in *italics*)

I am the owner of real estate located at 123 Main Street. It is my intent to enter into an agreement with [*your name here*] (hereinafter referred to as "Buyer"), on the following terms:

1. I will sign an Option agreement and related documents giving Buyer the legal right to lease and/or buy my property.

2. Sales price to be $35,000.

3. Length of time for Buyer to exercise Option to be: [*Negotiable. Three years or more is ideal. This is if you are doing an option. If not, take out.*]

4. Buyer has the right to lease my property for the monthly amount of $_____. [*This can also be a purchase amount.*]

5. Seller will prepare all documents at his/her expense to finalize this transaction.

6. I understand it is Buyer's intention to find another buyer to purchase the property and assign the purchase contract for a fee. I agree to allow Buyer to put a sign in the yard, and advertise the property for sale.

This is a Letter Of Intent and is not binding. If these terms are acceptable to Buyer, he/she will prepare documents that are legally binding to be signed by the parties.

Signed this _____ day of _____, 20___.
Seller _____
Seller _____

As you can see, the Letter of Intent is a simple form that only a serious seller will fill out. Once the form is filled out, you can begin marketing the property to your list of investor buyers!

The DM explains...

Some brand new investors worry that the Letter of Intent commits them to purchasing the property. But it doesn't! If you can find an investor-buyer who wants you to wholesale the deal to them then the LOI gives you the power to do so. However, if you can't find an investor-buyer who wants the deal, that's okay because the third point in the form gives you an "exit clause", allowing the deal to expire after a certain period of time.

This document is the real power behind wholesaling! It helps you to get the property under your control without you using your own money to buy the property!

The DM's Action Steps From This Chapter

1. Bookmark the key websites you'll use to perform your initial due diligence.

2. Gather the forms together that you'll need. (The forms are in the Appendix of the book. You can also find downloadable versions of these forms at www.VirtualRealEstateMadeEasy.com/forms).

"If you greatly desire something, have the guts to stake everything on obtaining it"

- Brendan Francis

CHAPTER 8

HOW TO WHOLESALE DEALS TO YOUR LIST (HINT: THIS IS WHERE IT ALL COMES TOGETHER!!!)

Florence, Italy, 6:42 PM
Writing from the balcony of my villa overlooking the vineyards

Although this might be the time most people eat supper, in Italy there is still an hour or two before anyone eats. So I'm maximizing my time before Deena and I head out, and I thought it might be a good time to write another chapter.

So I'm sitting here on the balcony of our villa and staring out over the red roofs of the city of Florence and all the vineyards. Just before starting to write, I wholesaled a property to an investor-buyer on my list.

In just a couple of quick back-and-forth emails, we covered the few details that needed to be covered. I'll make around seven thousand from the comfort of this scenic balcony. We still have some paperwork to sign but the deal is nearly complete, and it was all done virtually.

When people hear about one closed deal after another, they wonder how it's possible to do it all virtually. Here I am, writing to you from Florence, and I'm about to show you how.

In a previous chapter, I've showed you what you need to do virtually to get a property under control. In this chapter, I'm going to show you how you can wholesale the deal to an investor-buyer on your list.

Putting The Pieces Together

If you've followed the simple process I outlined in the last chapter to get a property under contract, now you're wondering what to do with that property. You're thinking, "Okay, DM, show me how to make money from that property!"

To get to this point, you need to make a couple of assumptions:

- You signed a Letter of Intent (LOI) to get the property under control while you do your due diligence.

- You've already done your virtual due diligence to make sure that the property is appropriate for you to wholesale to the investor-buyers on your list.

- You have an Option to Purchase form signed by the seller.

- And, you have a list of investor-buyers! (Of course you can market the deal online but the smartest, fastest, and easiest way to go is to market it to the list of investor-buyers you've been building)

You've got that contract in your hands (virtually speaking, of course) and you're wondering "What do I do now?"

Well, I'll show you but before I do, I want to point something out: Some will read this and get caught up in the details (there aren't many but there are a couple) and it will keep you from becoming virtual wholesalers. So here's what I want to remind you of first: Just get your first deal underway. Just push forward even if you're not 100% confident in the process get that first deal done and under your belt. Every time you do a deal, it will become faster and easier for you and your team. Every success (and every failure – because sometimes you might have a couple of those) will teach you something that will make you better next time.

So read this chapter and then please go out and do it. Put it into practice and see it at work.

Now let's look at how to communicate with your list and get those deals done…

Present The Deal To Your Investor-Buyers

Now it's time to tell your investor-buyers about the property you have available. And it's at this point that you'll see the value of building a list of investor-buyers first – before you find a deal – instead of after you find a deal (which is the way many wannabe real estate investors do it).

Instead of contacting one investor-buyer at a time and asking each one if they'd like to do the deal, you simply tell all of them at once about your deal and let only the interested ones get in touch with you.

I'll show you two ways to broadcast out to your investor-buyers quickly.

Email: The first and most straightforward way to get the word out to your investor-buyers is to use the same email system you've been using to build a relationship with them.

By now, they are used to getting emails from you and you've developed a rapport with them – they know a little about you and they trust you. So you can send them an email to tell them about the great property you've just got under contract.

Write one email, send it out, and wait for the interested ones to respond. I'll talk more about this a little later in the chapter, but first I want to give you an example of what to say to your investor-buyers (because this is important and can make or break your results)

You don't have to word every deal email like this one but just remember that you have a list of investor-buyers and think about what they are interested in knowing, and then mention those points in your email. Keep it brief and high-level, sharing only enough information to invite the interested investor-buyers to learn more (while weeding out the ones who aren't immediately able to make a deal).

For example, if your investor-buyers are primarily rehabbers, make sure you let them know what kind of rehab is required and how much they can increase the value of the home with their rehab. You don't have to give them an exact breakdown YET but you will want to tickle their greed glands.

Or, if your investor-buyers like to rent or lease-to-own, then make sure that you let them know why this property is perfect for tenants (i.e. ease of management, turnkey, ideal rental market, etc.)

So your email might look something like one of the two examples I've provided below.

Email example #1:

Hey! Want to make an easy $1,100 or more each month?

I just found a deal I think you'll be interested in. It's a 3 bedroom, 2 bathroom home in an area of Atlanta that is really growing.

Like all the homes in the neighborhood, this one is less than 15 years old and it is ready to rent. A lot of families are moving into the area because of some new businesses that just opened up.

Rents are $1,100 to $1,400. Interested in learning more?

Email me and let me know... but hurry

because this one is hot and it's not going to last long, It's going to our VIP buyers list so if you're interested let me know ASAP.

[Your Signature]

Email example #2:

Get a 3 bdrm 2 bath house in Atlanta that is turn-key with a tenant in place. Do nothing and make money.

Will go fast. Contact me NOW if you can pull the trigger after you see the facts.

Investor money available for this deal and can make up to 28% ROI.

By the way, you can use cash or IRA money too.

Email me now to get the details.

[Your Signature]

See how simple that was? You just write out some of the details that will capture the attention of your investor-buyers (get their greed glands going!) and you invite them to get in touch with you for more information or if they're interested. (Plus you remind them that you're sending it out to a whole bunch of people so they'd better act fast).

Then you just go golfing, or to the beach, or just go back to bed and when you get done playing or sleeping you will have some responses. If you've built a good relationship with your investor-buyers, and if you have a growing list of buyers, and if you wrote a compelling email, you should hear back from some of them. (By the way, if you don't hear back from very many of them, don't worry. Send out an email on this deal again or do another deal).

Have your virtual assistant keep close watch on your email inbox to handle any of the replies you get from your investor-buyers: When an email comes in, your assistant sends the prospective investor-buyer a nice flyer presentation of the deal and lets them know that this deal will go quickly so they should respond with questions and/or give us a thumbs up on moving forward.

Email is one way to get in touch with your investor-buyers and let them know about your deals but it's not the only way. If you're just getting started and you want to take action quickly without committing to too many different systems then it's the best way to get a fast start. But there's another way I really like…

Phone broadcast. As you collect a list of investor-buyers, invite them to give you their telephone number. Then, when you have a deal, call them using an automated phone broadcast system. It's a way to call a whole bunch of people at once and when they answer the phone, they hear your voice speaking.

Here's how it works: You simply record yourself speaking a message as if you were talking to someone, then upload that message to the phone broadcast system (there are a bunch out there but I use one at www.CallToProfits.com).

The system does the rest: It dials each number on your list and, when someone answers or if the voicemail picks up, the phone system automatically plays the recorded message from you, but it sounds real!

So, what kind of message should you record? Like the email you send to your list, keep it brief and high-level, sharing only enough information to invite the interested investor-buyers to learn more (while weeding out the ones who aren't immediately able to make a deal). You might say something like…

It's Mark Evans DM here. You expressed an
interest in doing some high profit real estate
deals recently. If you want to make an easy
$1,100 or more each month then you might be
interested in this great property in Atlanta. It's
a 3 bedroom, 2 bathroom family home in a
growing area of the city. It's ready to be lived
in and tenants are lining up for it.

If you want to learn more about how to make
$1,100 in rent each month from this deal, give
me a call at (123) 555-1234. Again my number
is: (123) 555-1234. If no answer, leave me a
message with your name and email and I'll
email more details to you.

I'll talk to you soon. Bye-bye …

Notice how simple that was! And remember: Keep it
virtual. Don't give out your own number; don't wait by the phone
for people to call. Instead, have your investor-buyers call your
virtual assistant's number (which you have already set up to go to
them) and provide a script to your assistant to field the calls; or
have the number go directly to a phone system that is just
voicemail-only. If you choose to have the number go directly to
voicemail, your message should be something like this:

Thank you for calling about the deal. We aren't
able to talk right now but I want to get you the
details as soon as possible so the best way for
me to do that is for you to leave your name, and
email (please spell your email out for me) and
I'll email you all the details. Again leave your
name and email address and remember to spell
it out and we'll shoot over the details to you

shortly. Thanks again for calling.

Bonus tip: Use Google Voice to get a free phone line if you need one. You can have someone answering the phone as well, but from my experience as your list grows, so will the calls coming in. If you send a message out like the one above, you might easily get 100-200 phone calls coming in, in only a few minutes! So an online answering machine is best. (Believe me, that's a great problem to have!)

No matter what you choose – email or phone broadcast or both – remember these tips to help you:

- Just whet their appetite to get in touch with you. Don't dump everything on them all at once. That's a rookie mistake!

- Keep in mind the kinds of things that interest your investor-buyers and present those things to them.

- Invite them to get in touch with you to learn more but remember to keep it virtual. Have your virtual assistant monitor your email and telephone for when people reply.

Now that I've given you a couple ways of getting in touch virtually with your investor-buyers, let's talk about some of the responses you'll get from them.

Responses You'll Get From Your Investor-Buyers

After sending out your email or phone broadcast (and/or both!) then it's time to go play and let the system do its thing. Actually, it's your virtual assistant's time to wait for responses and systems because you're too busy doing other things (like enjoying life and hanging out with your family and friends and doing the things you love to do).

So, what kind of responses can you expect? I'll cover some of them here. You'll want to let your virtual assistant know this information so that he or she can handle the email or phone calls appropriately.

No response: Although a flood of responses is the preferred result from your email or phone broadcast, the truth is that you might get no responses at all. (Depending on how many you're contacting) But that's okay! It happens. Fortunately, you aren't using any of your money to pay for a deal up-front so you haven't lost anything by presenting the deal to your investor-buyers.

Here are some reasons why it happens. If you don't get any responses from your email or phone broadcast, review these reasons and try again.

- You don't have enough investor-buyers. Presenting to investor-buyers is a numbers game: The more investor-buyers on your list, the more likely you are going to get a response. Although you can get started even with just a few investor-buyers, it's possible that the ones you have are actively investing elsewhere and maybe don't have the money at this exact moment. The best thing to do is always keep growing your list of investor-buyers. (Tip: Don't ever stop growing your list of investor-buyers! You'll thank me later if you actually do this).

- You don't have enough rapport with your investor-buyers. Building trust and rapport in a relationship takes time and interaction. And some people take longer to trust you than others. So if you invest the time to build a relationship with your investor-buyers over email, you're more likely to get a response when you present them with a deal. If you get no response on a particular deal, perhaps you just presented the deal to them too soon in the relationship. The best thing to do is keep building the relationship and keep presenting deals.

- Assuming you have people on your list, one of the biggest reasons that you don't get any responses is this one: You didn't present the property in a compelling way. You need to gain the attention of your investor-buyers quickly with a catchy headline that resonates with the things they're interested in. Yes, you might have a great deal but your investor-buyers are just like the rest of us: They're busy and they have a full inbox and they have to quickly weed through everything. If your email doesn't immediately capture their attention with your subject line (and only your subject line!) then they'll delete it and move on. Your relationship with them will help to address this but so will ensuring that your offer is clear and focused on the things that are of interest to them. The best thing to do is think about what will interest your investor-buyers and write those key points only in your email and then invite them to get in touch with you to learn more, you'll get better at this as you email them more often.

If you don't get any responses from your investor-buyers, don't worry about it. Wait 24 hours and try again: Change up the subject line and resend. Perhaps you just caught people on a day when they didn't open their email or maybe your email subject line wasn't enough to get them to open it. That's the great thing about using autoresponders and phone broadcast tools; you can change things up and try again on the fly.

And, if you don't get any traction on your deal, just shake it off and keep moving forward. It didn't cost you anything anyway. Learn from it and move on. Consider it a valuable (and free!) lesson in the state of your relationship with your investor-buyers.

Curious tire-kickers: As you grow a list of investor-buyers, some of them will be sophisticated investors who know exactly what they want and will only get in touch with you if they are ready to move forward. But others will be less sophisticated and will get in touch with you to learn more even if they don't have the money to move forward or turn out to be unable to commit to moving forward.

Please note: There's nothing wrong with these curious tire-kickers – they just aren't right for this exact deal. Don't offend them or remove them from your email list. However, train your virtual assistant to quickly identify the curious tire-kickers and get them out of the way to focus entirely on the legitimate and ready-to-move-forward investor-buyers.

Here's how to identify the tire kickers and deal with them by qualifying them on the phone: When they get a call, have them thank the caller and ask for their name and phone number and email. (This way, you can track who is calling and what they decide to do). Then have the assistant say something like: "I have a couple of questions for you as a potential buyer… This deal requires $XXXXXX. Are you able to meet that requirement?"

If the person is able to meet that requirement then move forward. If the person isn't able to meet that requirement at this time, your assistant should let them know if the deal qualifies for a self-directed deal (it can be bought using money from a self-directed IRA) and offer to get them some free information about using IRA's to purchase real estate.

In all the deals you do, time is of the essence and these deals can go quickly, so if an investor-buyer doesn't have the cash to do the deal right away, then the goal of the call switches and you just inform them about a way that they can get the cash to do future deals.

Either way (if they can do the deal or if they can't), make sure your virtual assistant leaves every caller better off when they called; and for investor-buyers who don't have the cash, you can help them by giving them insight for the future, so they will be ready on the next deal.

The ready-to-go investor-buyers: When you present a great opportunity to a list of interested investor-buyers who have a great rapport with you, you should hear back from some who are interested in learning more and are ready to move forward.

These are your top-tier responses and should be treated like gold! Have your virtual assistant answer their questions and help them to make a decision whether or not they want to do the deal with you. Remember: You don't actually need that many of these responses – you only need one!

When your virtual assistant gets a legitimate ready-to-go investor-buyer on the phone or on email, make sure your assistant has everything they need to move things forward so you can get on the phone with the investor-buyer and close the deal.

The DM explains...

Your virtual assistant's job is not to close the deals for you. Rather, your virtual assistant's job is to weed out the people who aren't serious and then send you a list of people who are serious about doing the deal. This is one of the most powerful differences between the way most real estate investors do it and the way a virtual real estate investor does it: Most real estate investors spend a lot of time on the phone going through call after call after call to try and find one interested investor-buyer. But a real estate investor who has set up their business to run virtually can have their virtual

*assistant spend their time weeding out the
callers so that only the most interested people
talk to the real estate investor. Imagine how
much more time you'll have (and how valuable
your time will be) when you only talk to
interested investor-buyers (because your
virtual assistant has narrowed the list for you).*

How To Communicate With Your Investor-Buyers

When your investor-buyers get in touch with your virtual assistant, make sure your virtual assistant has all the details they need. I use the cheat sheet called the Deal-at-a-Glance form. (See the Appendix for a copy of this form). I make sure it's filled out and that my virtual assistant has a copy. When the investor-buyer calls, just about everything they need is on this paper.

The virtual assistant's job is to do the following:

1. Ask some simple questions to determine whether the investor-buyer is serious or just a tire-kicker.

2. Use the Deal-at-a-Glance form to answer as many questions as possible for the investor-buyer.

3. Ask if they are ready to do the deal right away and offer to send the paperwork via fax or email.

4. Write down any questions they might have with a promise to get back to them within a specific timeframe.

5. Conclude the conversation with a firm

commitment to move forward even if the questions aren't fully answered.

6. Track down the answers to the questions immediately and respond to the investor-buyer.

The main thing to do throughout your communication is to keep the deal moving forward. So when investors first call, remind them that you have many buyers calling in and if they are serious about doing the deal, you'll send over the paperwork and you'll need a $1,000 deposit to hold the property while they do their due diligence. (The deposit will go against your fee if the deal goes ahead. If the deal doesn't go ahead, the deposit is refundable). I use Paypal for this.

If the investor-buyer is interested, the virtual assistant offers to send them the paperwork necessary. If the investor-buyer has basic additional questions, the virtual assistant handles those questions.

The investor-buyer will also probably want to do their own research and it's okay for the virtual assistant to give the information about the property to the investor-buyer.

Note: Some wholesalers worry that the investor-buyer will go behind their back and make an offer to the seller. Although this could theoretically happen, it's highly unlikely for the following reasons:

1. You already have a contract at this time – with the seller and with the investor-buyer (so contractually this is your deal).

2. You have done the hard work (at least in your investor-buyer's mind) of finding the deal so you are adding value to the deal.

3. Your investor-buyer would lose their prime

spot on your list of investor-buyers – they wouldn't get access to any more deals from you.

And remember: Throughout this entire exchange, you are sitting on the beach or hanging out at the cottage or traveling the world or gardening or playing with your kids – whatever you want. When an investor-buyer turns out to be ready (or on the odd occasion when your virtual assistant has a question they cannot answer on their own), you can handle the next step by email or Skype when you are ready.

How To Move Forward With The Deal And Get Paid

When your virtual assistant finds an investor-buyer who is interested in moving forward with the deal, your assistant needs to let the investor-buyer know how much the fee is to get the contract assigned to them. The investor buyer then sends the money to you – either through a certified check or Paypal or wire transfer (I prefer wire transfers). Then you fill out the Assignment form and send it to the investor-buyer. On the next page, I've provided an example of the Assignment form filled out. You can also find a blank example in the Appendix.

ASSIGNMENT AGREEMENT
(Example agreement with my explanations in *italics*)

This Agreement dated the <u>6th day of July, 2012</u> is made between <u>John Smith</u> [*this is the wholesaler*] (ASSIGNOR) and <u>Cindy Jones</u> [*this is the investor-buyer*] (ASSIGNEE), regarding the property described as:

The property address is known as <u>123 Main Street Anytown California, 12345</u> (SUBJECT PROPERTY)

WHEREAS, John Smith [*the wholesaler*] (ASSIGNOR) entered into a Purchase and Sales Agreement dated June 20th, 2012 with <u>Frank Williams</u> (SELLER) for the purchase of the SUBJECT PROPERTY, and whereas ASSIGNOR wishes to assign its rights and interest in the Purchase and Sales Agreement, it is hereby agreed between ASSIGNOR and ASSIGNEE as follows:

1. Assignment Fee. ASSIGNEE shall pay ASSIGNEE an assignment fee of <u>$10,000.00</u> [*the wholesaler's fee*] U.S. Dollars. Assignment fee is payable at close and shall not become due to ASSIGNOR until that time and unless title to SUBJECT PROPERTY is delivered to ASSIGNEE as per the terms of this contract and the Purchase and Sale contract.

2. Down Payment. ASSIGNEE shall pay <u>$3,000</u> U.S. Dollars of the Assignment Fee at the signing of this contract. The Down payment is refundable only if the Seller does not perform.

3. Closing Date. Closing is to take place on or before <u>July 25, 2012</u>.

4. Contract for Sale and Purchase Acknowledgement. ASSIGNEE accepts all terms and conditions of the original Contract for Purchase and Sale dated June 20th, 2012, in its entirety including

all addendums associated with this transaction.

5. Hold Harmless. ASSIGNOR shall not be held responsible for the performance of the ASSIGNEE, and shall further be held harmless for any other circumstances arising from or in connection with the SUBJECT PROPERTY or the Purchase and Sales Agreement.

6. Non Performance Acknowledgement. ASSIGNEE has read Paragraph S under Standards for Real Estate Transactions on the original Contract for Purchase and Sale and hereby agrees to abide by its terms. ASSIGNEE agrees that the terms of Paragraph S shall apply to all deposits and down payments tendered under this Agreement

7. Ownership and Property Access Acknowledgement. At the time of this Agreement, ASSIGNOR owns a contract for Purchase and Sale of SUBJECT PROPERTY, ASSIGNOR does not own title to the SUBJECT PROPERTY. ASSIGNOR and affiliated associates do not authorize ASSIGNEE to enter onto the SUBJECT PROPERTY. ASSIGNEE holds ASSIGNOR and associated affiliates harmless from liability arising from ASSIGNEE entering onto the SUBJECT PROPERTY,

8. Limitation of Assignment. It is hereby acknowledged by ASSIGNEE that this Agreement to Assign Contract for Sale and Purchase and the original Contract for Sale and Purchase are not assignable by ASSIGNEE without the express written authorization of ASSIGNOR, authorization of which may be withheld for any reason by ASSIGNOR

9. Additional Disclosures and Acknowledgements.
    a. Inspection Report and Subject Property Condition. Assignor and affiliated associates make no warranty express or implied regarding inspection reports, subject property condition or value or other reports provided to ASSIGNEE by ASSIGNOR or third parties concerning

this property. ASSIGNEE is advised to independently verify the accuracy of all information contained in reports concerning this property.

b. Real Estate Brokerage Disclosure. ASSIGNEE acknowledges they are conducting a transaction dealing directly with ASSIGNOR for the purchase of the SUBJECT PROPERTY. ASSIGNEE Is not relying on or being represented by a real estate brokerage in this transaction.

c. Affiliated Parties Disclosure. ASSIGNOR shall provide a statement of affiliated business arrangements. If any.

d. Lead Based Paint and Energy Efficiency Brochures. ASSIGNEE acknowledges receipt of Lead Paint and Energy Efficiency Brochures.

e. Entire Agreement This agreement constitutes the entire agreement and no modification 01 this Agreement shall be binding unless signed by the parties. No representation, promise or inducement not included in this agreement shall be binding upon any party hereto.

10. Additional Terms and conditions of this Agreement .are as follows:

AGREED AND ACCEPTED:

_____

ASSIGNOR   Date   ASSIGNEE   Date

_____

ASSIGNOR   Date   ASSIGNEE   Date

… And the deal is done.

Yes, that's it.

You get paid, you send the deal to the investor-buyer, and then you move on.

What did you notice about this entire exchange covered in the previous chapter and this chapter? I hope you noticed that it involved almost no effort on your part and yet still resulted in you receiving a check A.K.A. getting PAID!

Although I've laid it out with some additional tips and ideas, but overall you should notice just how easy it is: Your virtual assistant deploys the marketing to extract deals. Your virtual assistant does some due diligence to research the deals. Your virtual assistant works with the seller to get the deal under contract with your direction. Your assistant sends out an email to your list about the deal and/or they cue up the voice broadcast to let them know deal is hot. Then your virtual assistant interacts with investor-buyers. And then you get the money.

That's right! You get paid even though you did very little work to put it all together.

The DM explains…

I want to make one more thing very clear: You are giving your virtual assistant a lot of responsibility here but they are not actually doing the deal. You are. Your assistant does most of the administrative work and qualifies the sellers and the investor-buyers but you are the one who negotiates the deal with the seller and closes the deal with the investor-buyer. I mention this for two reasons: First, your virtual assistant is a very useful resource to have but you should use them only for the work you shouldn't do yourself (and a lot of the

activities in a real estate investing business
can be outsourced). Second, you don't want to
invite legal trouble by having someone else
doing the negotiation and closing the contract.
Keep that activity for yourself and the rest of
real estate investing is easy!

In the next chapter, I'm going to talk about the money you can make from virtual wholesaling.

"Too many people are thinking of security
instead of opportunity. They seem more afraid
of life than death."

- James F. Byrnes

The DM's Action Steps From This Chapter

1. Write out an example email to use as a template when you get a deal. (You can use the example I used earlier in this chapter; just change it for yourself).

2. Write out an example phone broadcast you can use as a template when you get a deal. (Again, you can use the example I used earlier in this chapter; just change it for yourself).

3. Gather the forms together that you'll need. (The forms are in the Appendix of the book. You can also find downloadable versions of these forms at www.VirtualRealEstateMadeEasy.com/forms).

"Every day you may make progress. Every step may be fruitful. Yet there will stretch out before you an ever-lengthening, ever-ascending, ever-improving path. You know you will never get to the end of the journey. But this, so far from discouraging, only adds to the joy and glory of the climb."

- Sir Winston Churchill

CHAPTER 9

THE MONEY CHAPTER

Anguilla, British West Indies AG. 5:43 am
Writing from a hammock on the beach

I travel a lot. I've been to some pretty amazing (and sometimes pretty crazy) places. I'm living the kind of life that most people are hoping to do in their retirement. People are trying to save for retirement so that they can stop working and start traveling (or spending their time how they want to spend their time). Instead of working now and saving for retirement, I've built a business that gives me the money to live that kind of life right now.

I want to show you how to do it. It's easier than you realize and I'm fortunate enough to have figured out how to make it happen now (instead of waiting until "retirement age").

In this chapter, I want to lay out all the money details for you and hopefully answer your burning financial questions.

Money! Everything Has Been Building Up To This!

This is the money chapter. It's a chapter that I assume some of you have turned to first before reading the rest of the book. That's okay (I'd do the same!) but if you're reading this first and you haven't read the rest of the book, you need to know something ahead of time:

Money is only part of the picture. Although we need money to pay our bills and fund our lifestyle, you'll read in the first couple of chapters that I place a higher importance on **"<u>time-freedom</u>"** and working to live the lifestyle you want to live.

And although the virtual wholesaling system I outline in this book is designed to potentially give you financial freedom, it's more importantly meant to give you the freedom to live the lifestyle you want to live.

What I mean is: There are many ways to make a ton of money but those other systems and processes and blueprints require a lot of work. Of course you'll have some work to do, even with what I'm describing here, but the secret I hope you're starting to pick up is: It's very important to be working on your business not just in it. Work once to build your business so you don't have to do as much work in the future.

With the virtual wholesaling system, I want to help you make enough money to afford your dreams but I also want to give you the time-freedom so you can do what you want, when you want, where you want!

Important Disclaimer

Before I go on, I need to make an important disclaimer: I'm going to be describing details about money in this chapter but not everyone is going to have the same result as the one I'm describing.

I'm sure it's not news to you that there are many factors that determine success: The virtual wholesaling system I've described in this book is a general blueprint that can help you achieve your lifestyle goals. But there aren't any guarantees in this book or in life for that matter. And just by reading this book, it doesn't assure you of success.

All I'm doing in this entire book (including this chapter) is outlining a system that has worked for me and helping you understand it so you can use it for yourself.

But the ultimate determinant of success is NOT my system, nor is it the market, nor is it the economy, nor is it the quality of your deals, or is it the quality of the investor-buyers; the ultimate determinant of success is...

... YOU.

Your success is entirely up to you – that includes your financial freedom, your time freedom, and your achievement of the lifestyle you've been dreaming of. It's all up to you.

So just like everything else in this book, use this chapter as a guideline and then go out and build a virtual wholesaling business that works for you.

Some readers are going to read this chapter, think about it for three hours, and then feel good that they have moved their real estate investing business forward. But that's not action. That is just thinking. You need to take action if you want to start making money.

The DM explains...

I'm talking a lot about money in this chapter but I want to make an important note: Almost nothing in life is guaranteed. Just because you read this book and implement it doesn't guarantee you will become successful. However, I've learned an important lesson: Taking action to move toward your goals is going to increase the likelihood that they'll come true. And if you decide to do nothing about your goals? Well, then it's almost guaranteed that those goals WON'T come true.

Got it? Good. Now let's talk about money...

How Much Can You Make?

This is the great, big million-dollar question. I get asked it all the time. "Hey DM, how much money can I make as a virtual wholesaler?"

My first answer usually annoys people (and if you read the disclaimer above then you can probably guess what my first answer is). My first answer is: "How much you make is entirely up to you."

Yeah, people don't like that answer very much. They want the numbers. So here are the numbers you're looking for (although they are approximate since there are some fluctuations):

On every wholesaling deal, you can stand to potentially make $1,000 to $15,000 in gross income. (And since your expenses are ridiculously low, that's a pretty-close-to-accurate profit number, too).

The difference between $1,000 and $15,000 is a pretty wide margin but it all depends on a few things, including:

- How many deals you've done. Early on, you might do some slightly lower-earning deals just to get the deals done. Later, you might bump up the price a little when you have more experience. (I think if you just do a deal and make zero in dollars, you still made more on the experience than you will ever make in $) The key is to get that first deal done.

- What kind of deals you do. A smaller property with a lower price might demand a lower fee added to it (compared to a higher-end property). Of course you want to maximize your profit on each deal but remember to leave enough meat on the deal for the investor buying from you.

- How strong of a negotiator you are. Remember, you'll be negotiating terms with sellers to get a great deal to offer to investor-buyers. So if you negotiate hard to get a low-priced deal, you might be able to ask for a higher fee from your investor buyers (compared to if you were able to get a deal but the price wasn't negotiated as low as you'd like).

Just like any other product or service – because that's what you're selling is a product (a property) and a service (finding a deal for your investor-buyers) – your market determines the price.

If you have a great deal and a great list of investor-buyers but no one bites on the deal when you offer it, try shaving a bit of money off of the deal and see what happens.

In general, aim for somewhere between $1,000 and $15,000 and your experience will help you find the right price. (Of course you can make a whole lot more than $15,000 but price ranges will reflect this number.)

I also want to mention that you might not earn between $1,000 and $15,000 per deal. I'm just telling you about the money from deals that I do. There are many factors that will influence the price. And just because you find a deal and an investor-buyer doesn't guarantee that you'll close the deal. For example, maybe it's a deal that your investor-buyers aren't looking for, or maybe you don't have quite enough investor-buyers to do the volume of deals you want to do. There are many factors and you might encounter some of them. But keep growing your business and doing deals.

I Can Hear It Now ... So How Much Can You Make???

Don't try to get me to lie to you. I'm not going to give you an exact dollar figure. I can't. Everyone has different sets of skills (such as private connections, good sales ability, maybe they have a pocket deal, maybe they have been studying for years already or are completely brand new). Everyone comes to this with different ideas about what is success. Ultimately, I can't give you a dollar figure because everyone is going to have a different experience.

But here's what I can tell you: Earlier in the chapter I gave you a range of $1,000 to $15,000 (or more) per deal. And I realize that you don't want to know how much you can make on one deal; you want to know how much you can make if you replace your current career with virtual wholesaling.

Well, I have another answer for you that might not be what

you expect. My answer is "Figure out how much your current expenses are and do enough deals to cover your expenses." By doing this, you get the time-freedom you want because you no longer have to work your 9-5 job to pay for your expenses. You can stay home or travel or hang out on the golf course knowing full well that your expenses are covered.

Let me give you an example: Let's say that your current total household expenses are $2,500 per month – that's all of your food, your utilities, your mortgage payment and your car payments.

And let's say that you can do a deal and make $5,000.

Simple math tells us that you will need to do around 6 deals in a year in order to pay your monthly bills and enjoy the time-freedom you want.

To the total newbie, 6 deals in a year can seem like an almost overwhelming number, so let's break it down a bit more:

That's just one deal every two months. That means, every 60 days, you need to...

1. Instruct your virtual assistant to advertise for a new property. (He or she will weed through the deals and find some that have potential).

2. Choose a few of properties. (Your virtual assistant perform further due diligence) and work with sellers to negotiate terms that will make an attractive deal to your investor-buyers.

3. Present the deal to your list of investor-buyers.

4. Cash the check when an investor-buyer pays your fee to get the assignment.

Do you think you can do those things in 60 days? Of course you can! Many virtual wholesalers can do several of those activities in a week so doing just one deal in 60 days to cover your monthly expenses is simple to do.

Using these above numbers as assumptions (and remember, it's going to be different for everyone), here's what one virtual wholesaler might make. Think of this as a case study example to illustrate how the numbers work:

To cover their monthly expenses of $2,500, the virtual wholesaler decides to do one deal every two months. However, after the first deal, they realize just how easy it is so they decide to do one deal a month. Instead of $30,000/year ($5,000 x 6 months), they earn $60,000/year ($5,000 x 12 months). After all, it doesn't really take them very much time at all. Later, as their confidence grows, they might increase this to two deals a month or even one deal a week.

And, as they grow the number of deals they're doing, something else is happening: They are increasing the number of investor-buyers they are connected with, they are deepening their relationship with investor buyers, and they are honing their marketing and sales skills. In other words, it's not just the number of deals that increases but the overall components that make up a successful real estate business... and when that happens, you can potentially make more money faster.

The DM explains...

I just said that you could potentially make more money faster by improving the components of your real estate investing business. That's because you'll be building your base of investor-buyers so when you have a deal, there will be more investor-buyers who may want to do the deal with you. And, you'll be deepening your relationships with investor buyers so they'll trust you more and they'll be willing to do even more deals with you because they feel like they know you. And as you improve your marketing and sales skills, you'll be able to find more deals and investor-buyers, negotiate more skillfully, and close more often. So when you combine all of those components, your real estate investing business grows even when you're not doing deals every day (as long as you work at growing your business).

So, to answer your question about how much money you can make, it all depends on you and how much you want to earn. I've given you some financial estimates and you need to figure out how much you want to make and that will help you estimate how many deals to do.

Don't Be Greedy

I'm adding in this quick note – don't be greedy – because some virtual wholesalers might look at the $1,000 to $15,000 fee and think: "Why not make it $20,000 or more?".

But the important thing to remember is that you aren't selling to consumers or retail buyers. You are selling to someone who is hoping to turn around and make some money off the deal, too.

So if you sell at too high of a fee, you are potentially taking some of your investor-buyer's profit off the table. By putting your fee too high, you reduce your chances of selling your properties (because the investor-buyers won't see the profit-potential for themselves).

$1,000 to $15,000 is a good range to aim for and you'll learn soon enough how much to charge, although it's all relative because you can make more on a $1 million property compared to a $100,000 property.

Bonus idea: You could even do a bidding war with potential buyers and let them bid it up. Let's say you get three buyers who each want the deal. You can do a telecall or a webinar with them all and have them bid against each other like an auction.

Who knows, your $500,000 deal could go to $545,000 or even $700,000! That's the beauty of this business; you never know what will happen but the key is you have options and your options increase as you get more experienced.

Are Your Fees Negotiable?

Everything in life is negotiable. Remember that! As you get more experienced, you'll find new opportunities in negotiation. But in the beginning, find a fee you're comfortable charging that is low enough to ensure everyone in the deal wins. If someone asks you to lower your fee, consider lowering it if it means you do the deal and everyone (including you) still wins.

You need to find the balance between doing what is necessary to do the deal and giving away too much. Plus, although negotiation is okay, you don't want to set a precedent by lowering your fee just because someone asks.

I've seen some wholesalers get stuck on a number (like $5,000) and then they get upset when someone asks to do the deal for only $1,000. Always check to make sure it's a win for you (it can still be a win at a lower amount) and for everyone else.

And my most important advice: On your first deal, just get that deal closed even if you break even on it because the experience will be worth so much more.

How To Be Paid

The simplest way to get paid is by wire into your bank account. It's fast (clears in a couple hours). It's also safe because you can make sure the money clears before you send the paperwork.

At first, just stick with this simple, straightforward way. Later on, you might consider adding additional ways to get paid but I don't want to bog you down with details. Just get them to wire you the money or get you a bank (certified) check and put it in your account – you don't need to make it more complicated than that!

But there are other ways to transact money. You might consider accepting credit cards or Paypal.

These methods have their advantages and disadvantages but my main concern is that you just get started and wires and bank checks are the fastest and easiest way to do that.

But Wait, There's More!

This chapter is the money chapter but there is something else I absolutely must cover. It has to do with the value of your time.

Everything has value – the amount of time you spend at work is valued at your wage (I mean: You trade those 8 hours of the day for a certain amount of money).

So as you think about living the lifestyle of your dreams, it's important to remember that your potential income is only part of the equation. Money coming in is good – but so is the freedom that comes from not "spending" your valuable time to make that money.

Work Once And Get Paid Over And Over!

Do you get what I'm saying? Let me give you an example: If I offered you $1,000, you might be interested. But that $1,000 would seem way more valuable if I just handed it to you without you having to work for it versus if I handed you a pitchfork and asked you to spend the weekend cleaning out a dirty barn.

The $1,000 earned without a lot of ongoing work is actually worth more because there was no ongoing time investment to get it. (Sure, you invested a bit of time to set everything up but if you do it correctly, you only do it once and you can profit from it again and again).

It's the same with virtual wholesaling. Even if you just

start out earning enough money to cover your monthly expenses, and not a penny more, that money is vastly more valuable because you earned it without actually doing a lot of work for it (compared to earning the same money by showing up to your 9-5 job every day).

Be very conscious of your time spent actually working. Use a journal to record the amount of time you spend. Of course, in the beginning it always takes some time to set things up (plus you don't really move as quickly when you're tentatively starting out) but as you get it set up and get things going you'll see your time on the business increases while your time in the business drops drastically... Even to the point you may start getting bored. (It's true! Ask some retirees you know if they got bored when they had money coming in without working. Why do you think so many retired people go back out and find a job after retirement?)

"The greatest discovery of my generation is that a human being can alter his life by altering his attitudes of mind."

- William James

The DM's Action Steps From This Chapter

1. Determine your financial freedom goal by adding up all of your monthly expenses (i.e. mortgage, telephone, cable, car payments, etc.). This is the amount of money you need to earn from virtual wholesaling to never have to work again. So invest time on this and make sure to include your fun money.

2. Set up a journal to record how you spend your time. Although you might put in a bit more time at the beginning to set up your business, you should make the conscious effort later to pull back from the "hands-on" aspect of running your business (make the decision to switch from working in your business to working on your business).

"Believe in yourself! Have faith in your abilities! Without a humble but reasonable confidence in your own powers you cannot be successful or happy"

- Norman Vincent Peale

PART 3

AFTER YOU GET STARTED, HERE'S WHAT YOU NEED TO KNOW...

In Part 1, I introduced you to the world of real estate investing and, specifically, to wholesaling. I told you why I thought virtual wholesaling was the fastest, easiest way to achieve the success you desire in life.

In Part 2, I let you step by step through the key components of a virtual wholesaling business, and I showed you how to put it all together so that it runs almost on autopilot (as long as you work on your business and not in your business).

In Part 3, I now want to help you get moving forward and take your virtual wholesaling business to the next level. I'm going to show you how to grow your business more, I'll reveal some advanced tips and ideas that you don't need to implement right away but they'll be there when you're ready, and be sure to read the most important chapter in the book which tells you the one crucial lesson that everything in this book hinges on.

"There will always be a seemingly valid reason NOT to do something. There will always seem to be a better time, place, or circumstance. But most people find that the perfect time never actually arrives. A day can so easily turn into a decade with the activities and responsibilities of life. But to those who truly want to make a change, there is always time."

- The DM

CHAPTER 10

BECOMING A SUCCESSFUL REAL ESTATE INVESTOR AND ACHIEVING YOUR DREAMS IN LIFE

St Bart's, French West Indies, 7:19 AM
Writing from beach

I'm sitting here, looking at an unbelievable view of the ocean. It's going to get much hotter today but right now it's still pretty nice out so I thought I'd do some writing before it got too hot.

It seems like only yesterday I did my first wholesale deal and thought to myself, "whoa, this is incredible." It was the easiest money I've ever made at that time. I had struggled through other types of real estate investing and nearly gone bankrupt twice. But this deal was different. It took a little amount of work to set up but I basically just followed the steps I've outlined in the book with some minor adjustments. (Disclaimer: My first deals were actually old school deals where I showed the property. But since then, I've gone completely virtual with my wholesale business and those lessons are what I'm sharing with you).

But if I had stopped at that first deal, where would I be? Well, I probably wouldn't be writing my sixth published book from the beach!

And if I had not pushed myself to break the old ways of thinking and adopt a virtual mindset, where would I be? Well, I probably wouldn't be on a 5-year trip around the world.

In this chapter I want to talk about what happens after you do your first deal – how to move beyond that initial euphoric success to build a virtual wholesaling business that continues to grow while you spend time with your family or friends, doing the things you love in the places you've always dreamed of visiting.

Moving Beyond The Facts: Here's How To Go From Knowledge To Action

At this point in the book, I've given you everything I think you need to start your own virtual wholesaling business. I've shown you the importance of building your list of investor-buyers and building a relationship with them, I've showed you how to find deals and share those deals with your list, and I've talked about money. And most importantly, I've shown you how to do it all virtually.

In a way, I've laid out a business plan in an almost step-by-step process for you to follow to get everything set up and to get deals going. And in this chapter, I want to talk about how you can grow your business to become even more successful.

(Before I do that, though, I want to make a quick reminder about what I mean when I say "successful". I don't mean that you'll necessarily add a million dollars to your bank account. Only you can define what success means to you, and virtual wholesaling has the potential to give you the time-freedom and financial-freedom to achieve that success. But it's all up to you and whether you're willing to take action.)

So, let's talk about what you need to do to grow your business and become successful.

Just GET STARTED

One of the biggest points that trip up many aspiring real estate investors is that they read a lot about how to start a real estate investing business and do every type of investing strategy but they don't actually do anything about it. They turn into "7-year newbies", which is something I've mentioned in a previous chapter.

So the most important thing is to just get started and work through your first deal. Once you do that, you'll have enough information to move forward and grow your business rapidly.

When I started wholesaling, my goal was to just to get through the first deal. Although I wanted to ultimately be a virtual wholesaler, I wanted to watch the process close-up and see how it all worked. I wanted to have a virtual assistant in place but I also wanted to (virtually) peek over their shoulder to watch what they did. Frankly, I didn't even care about whether or not I made a profit on the first deal. I considered the deal to be my education in working out the kinks of the process and making sure that I understood it enough so that I could manage it no matter where I was.

I urge you to do the same thing. Most people who never leave the "aspiring" stage to become actual real estate investors are held back because they just don't get started.

So if you're serious about becoming a virtual wholesaler, just get started. Just push forward. Just get that first deal done and see how it works.

Do it in chunks; go for small victories. Some examples are:

- Find a virtual assistant

- Place an advertisement to get real estate investors

- Get your email autoresponder set up

See? It doesn't have to be all huge steps. You can move your virtual wholesaling business forward by working on one small chunk and then another and then another. Before you know it you'll be standing there with a check in your hand smiling ear-to-ear.

Once you've done that, you can officially call yourself a real estate investor. And now here's the best part: Once you've done your first deal, it becomes so easy to simply…

Repeat Over And Over And Over And Over

Once you've done the first deal, every other deal becomes easier and easier. So once you've done the first deal, analyze what you liked about it and didn't like about it and make notes and don't make that mistake again and then go do another deal.

Remember how you felt when you first got behind the wheel of a car to learn to drive? If you were like most teens, you probably felt a mix of excitement and fear. But how is your driving now? You probably do it every day without giving it a second thought.

It's the same with virtual wholesaling. That first deal can be scary (even though I've showed you exactly how to do it with little effort on your part). But every time you "get behind the wheel" and do it again, each deal becomes easier.

And easier.

And easier.

And easier!

Just a few deals later, you'll be an old pro, and you'll look back from your beach house or from the back nine of your favorite golf course and you'll remember back to that point when you were initially fearful of starting but you did it anyway and laugh about it.

The key is to get through that first deal and then don't stop.

For the virtual wholesalers who do their first deal and then stop (perhaps relieved that they got through it but fearful of repeating because they don't realize that the fear goes away just like driving a car), they miss out on a key aspect of wholesaling. It's called cash flow…

Cash Flow – A Magic Word You Need To Remember

Virtual wholesaling brings in a nice hit of cash; somewhere between $1,000 and $15,000, depending on your deals. Everyone loves getting a bucket of cash like that added to

164

their bank account all at once.

And although getting that money once is a great thing, it only goes so far.

Between mortgage payments and the kid's braces and that dream vacation, your first deal's income can slowly get spent. (No problem! That's what it's there for).

So a spike in income is nice but what virtual wholesalers need to stay in business is cash flow. Cash flow is basically an ongoing stream of money coming into your account – it's a flow of cash.

I don't want to bore you with the details but accountants, investors, and financial experts frequently say that cash flow is one of the most important aspects of any business (not just a real estate investing business) and it's even more important than just a high profit.

So, you are a virtual wholesaler if you do one deal but the life you dream of living won't last very long on that one deal. What you need is consistent cash flow.

Cash flow comes from doing more deals – from repeating your first deal again and again and building a real estate business that generates you more cash flow.

The Three Most Important Things

The best way to build your business and repeat your deals over and over (to generate that all-important cash flow) is to do three things. If you do these three things, it will assure your future as a successful virtual wholesaler.

How important are these three activities? Well, in the virtual wholesaling part of my business (because I make other kinds of deals, too), I consider these three things to be the keys to my success.

If you only focus on these three things for the rest of your life, your virtual wholesaling business will naturally grow:

1. Grow your list of investor-buyers

2. Build your relationship with them
    consistently

3. Sell them deals

If you focus only on these three things, your virtual wholesaling business will grow because, as you've seen, finding the deals and presenting them to your list is actually a small, easy part of the process that is almost entirely done by your virtual assistant while you hang out on your back deck with your friends (or do whatever else you want to do).

So, when aspiring virtual wholesalers ask me, "Hey DM, I really want to dominate as a virtual wholesaler, what should I become an expert in?" my answer is always the same: Learn how to relentlessly grow a list of investor-buyers and build a tight-knit relationship with them and provide them with the deals they want.

Do those things and your future success (however you define it) is clearly charted.

Keep It Really Simple

One of the takeaways I hope you've discovered while reading this book is just how simple everything really is. There really isn't a lot of work, relativity speaking, IF you build it properly and always work on your business and the work that is done can be repeated by an assistant (so it allows you to build a business and enjoy life).

I sometimes joke that virtual wholesaling is the lazy way to success. (Of course I'm just joking – it's not laziness; it's building a smart real estate investing business that doesn't require you to be doing all the pieces). In reality, I think every business owner should pay attention to their business 24/7 but that doesn't mean they need to be doing hands-on work 24/7. That's a big difference!

So one of the lessons I hope to instill in you is this: Keep it simple. Don't let it get complicated. Use the easy process I've described and do it over and over again. I sometimes joke that you need to "keep things boring". Of course I don't mean that you should actually get bored, I just mean you should make things so easy and repetitive that they can be done on autopilot while you spend most of your time doing something else.

As you become more successful, you might be tempted to make it more complicated than it needs to be. Although there are advanced techniques (which I'll talk about in an upcoming chapter), you don't need to adopt these techniques. If you only do what I've described throughout this book, you'll be moving in the right direction to building a business that can run virtually while you do the things you love to do.

You've heard of the "KISS principle" (Keep it Simple, Stupid). Well, it applies here. After all, the fewer moving parts you have in your business, the easier it is to work on your business from anywhere in the world.

Work On Your Business, Not In Your Business

I realize I've written this before but it bears repeating. There will be times throughout the early months of your virtual wholesaling business when you are tempted to stop working on your business and start working in it. Perhaps you'll look at what you're paying for virtual assistant (even though it's not very much) and think that you could save that money by doing their work yourself. Or maybe you end up on the phone with an investor-buyer and you think "Hey, I should just give out my phone number more often".

It's natural that you'll feel that way because you and everyone else has been raised with the idea that you have to show up and work hard in order to be successful. And worse yet, your friends and family might even tell you that you might be more successful if you actually did the work yourself instead of outsourcing it.

I urge you to fight that temptation! You are doing yourself

a disservice by choosing to go from virtual wholesaling to "non-virtual" wholesaling. You're giving up the freedom you could have and simply taking on a job.

I predict that you'll need to fight this feeling for 6 months to a year. But after that, you'll realize that life is so much sweeter when you're running a virtual wholesaling business. After that, you'll understand the importance of what you're learning here.

The DM explains...

I've been describing a virtual real estate investing system to give you the freedom to do what you want. But there's something you might notice (which I also notice in my own real estate investing business). Even though you should strive to work on your business instead of in your business, you might have skills and interests that you want to put to good use in your business. Of course there's nothing wrong with doing that. But the virtual real estate investing system I'm describing in this book gives you the freedom to do what you want – travel or hang out with your kids or sit on your back deck or lay on the beach or use your skills in your real estate investing business. The key is that you have the freedom to do what you want.

Always Strive For Win/Win

Another way to grow your business is to adopt the principle of win/win. Frequently when aspiring real estate investors see what kind of money they could make from virtual wholesaling, they start tacking zeros onto the end of each potential fee they charge. Or they grind down their already-inexpensive virtual assistants to accept an even lower rate.

Although every business owner should maximize profit

Virtual Real Estate Investing Made Easy

(regardless of whether you're in virtual wholesaling or in some other business), remember that you will be more successful when you help other people around you to become successful as well.

If you leave a little extra money on the table for your investor-buyers (so they pay you a fair price but make a fair profit themselves) then you'll have happy investor-buyers who are eager to do more deals with you. And if you pay your virtual assistants what they are worth then you'll have loyal assistants who will go the extra mile for you.

When you help other people win, you win too.

Just Get Going!!!

Your virtual wholesaling business doesn't have to be perfect. I don't try to hide that my business is far from perfect. But I make sure all the important pieces are moving in the right direction.

I always say: "Just remember, you don't have to get it right you just have to get it going".

And when someone comes up with an excuse as to why they cannot do it now, I always ask: "If not now, when?"

169

The DM's Action Steps From This Chapter

1. If you use a calendar on your computer or smartphone, schedule in time to build your list of investor-buyers every day.

2. If you use a calendar on your computer or smartphone, schedule in time to build your relationship with your investor-buyers every day.

3. If you use a calendar on your computer or smartphone, schedule in time to present deals to your investor-buyers regularly. (It might not be every day at first but you should aim to do something significant at least once a week to do a deal. You can always increase the frequency later).

"A goal without a plan is just a wish."

- Antoine de Saint-Exupery

CHAPTER 11

ADVANCED IDEAS – SUCCEED WITH THESE IDEAS ONCE YOUR REAL ESTATE INVESTING BUSINESS IS BOOMING!

London, England. 11:35 pm
Writing from a café beside the London Bridge

Today I was in a restaurant, enjoying dinner with some people that Deena and I had met earlier this week. They were vacationers – they had each taken time off of work to come here for some time off. As their vacation was winding up, they admitted to Deena and I that they weren't looking forward to returning to the rat race.

As we were telling each other about what we do for a living, they were surprised to discover that Deena and I are on a 5 year trip and they wondered how complicated it was to run a business that allowed it to happen.

I try not to talk business while enjoying dinner but this couple was adamant about learning how I work virtually and can travel while I run my business.

Part way through the conversation, the guy said that he assumed it was probably too complicated for someone else to replicate – that there were too many advanced aspects that required technological savvy and a huge amount of capital... or even if it was a scam.

Nothing could be further from the truth and I briefly (without boring them, I hope) described how simple it was to do.

By the end of the evening, as we shook hands and said goodbye, I think I still detected a look of skepticism in their eyes. I hope that when they return to the US, they look up my website and do some research to discover that it is just as simple as I've described. In fact, a lot of people look at me like I'm from another planet when they learn about what I do. It's so unusual to most people and it's one of the reasons that I'm writing this book – I want people to know that it's possible and within reach of almost anyone who wants to do it.

"But DM... What You've Described Is TOO EASY!!!"

When aspiring people first hear about the virtual wholesaling, it often seems almost too simple. That's because almost everyone has been raised with the idea that you have to show up and work hard to achieve success.

But it really is simple and in this book I've explained how easy it can be.

My goal with this book has been to lay out everything you need to know so that you can put down the book and actually go out and succeed as a virtual wholesaler. I've tried to be as clear and direct as possible, showing you how to set up your wholesaling business so that it runs virtually and gives you the freedom you deserve.

Too many people assume that there are roadblocks, or they allow the unfamiliar aspects of setting up a virtual wholesaling business to become roadblocks. But if you simply follow what I've written, you'll discover that setting everything up is extremely easy, and running your virtual wholesaling business can be just as easy.

And, in a previous chapter I warned you not to make it too complicated on yourself. I don't want you to give up the lifestyle that you are trying to achieve by becoming a virtual wholesaler!

But with that said, I do want to point out that there are advanced techniques and tactics that you can do to help you become even more successful.

But here's an important point for me to make: **Don't read any further until you've already set up your virtual wholesaling business!** Don't let the content you read here keep you from setting up a simple virtual wholesaling business.

Set it up then come back to this chapter and read through it to make your business more advanced if you want to.

I'll list a few advanced tactics that I think you might want to consider for your business.

Sorting Your List

As you build up your list of investor-buyers, you're going to discover a few things about them. For example, you'll discover...

- Some of the people on your list are really responsive and very interested in investing. And when you present a deal, they jump on it and want to throw money at you and your deals.

- Some of the people on your list are responsive because they like the idea of being an investor-buyer but they never actually buy anything.

- Some of the people on your list are a certain kind of investor-buyer – perhaps only interested in properties they can rent or properties they can lease or properties they can rehab; or perhaps only interested in properties in a certain geographic region; or perhaps only interested in properties that are multi-families buildings, etc. Your job as you grow your list is to extract this important information so you can send the best deals to your list. (One way to do this is with a survey you can have your new investor-buyers fill out. I've included a copy of the survey in the Appendix.

Virtual Real Estate Investing Made Easy

- And some of the people on your list just don't say anything ever. They don't reply to your questions, they don't always open your emails, they never make any offers.

When you sort your list of subscribers, you can send your emails to everyone, but once in a while you might find that you want to send it to only a small group of people. For example, if you find that a bunch of people on your list of investors are big into rehabbing, you might send a rehab deal to only those investors (instead of sending it out to your entire list). This is called segmenting.

Sometimes when I tell new real estate investors this concept, it surprises them because they are used to the idea of blasting out a huge broadcast of marketing. But a small, highly-targeted, responsive list can oftentimes be much more lucrative than a large list.

There are some advantages to this:

- You become even more valuable to your list because people start to see things that only they are interested in.

- You can start to weed out the tire-kickers who are always interested in learning more but never willing to move forward. (Never be rude to these people but also don't waste your time with long, detailed email replies to their many questions – give them quick answers and focus on the people who are more likely to work with you). A more advanced technique is to sell information to these people. These tire-kickers aren't ready to invest in deals but they are probably interested in learning more about investing. Many real estate investors make seven figures

174

a year just helping tire-kickers become more informed.

- You can also generate even more urgency by only releasing a deal to a small group of your most responsive investor-buyers.

- You can also test your emails by sending out the deal to half of your list, and then rewriting the email and sending the same deal (through a re-written email) to the other half of your list, to find out which email prompted the greater response. Tracking!

- You can also email people who are in a certain area to let them know if you happen to be in the area – it's a great way to build your relationships further with your investor-buyers.

By sorting your list into groups of people, you deepen the relationship and can improve the likelihood that you'll do a deal. It can also reduce the amount of time that your virtual assistant spends answering replies because you're sending the email to a smaller group of more targeted investor-buyers.

Of course, you should still always email your full list of investor-buyers regularly (I believe you should email them at least once a week) in order to build the relationship and to give everyone the opportunity to do deals with you. But there are times when targeting a smaller group of people will increase the likelihood of a deal so splitting your list into groups is a good idea.

Cash Flow – Two Of The Sweetest Words In Real Estate Investing

If you follow all of the steps in this book and you do one deal, that's great! You're well on your way. But you've only just begun. One deal will get you closer to your dream but, of course, one deal alone won't let you quit your job and travel the world (or do whatever it is you dream about doing when you have financial freedom).

What you want is an ongoing, regular flow of income ("cash flow" is the lingo in the real estate investing world) to keep money coming in.

There are a few ways to create cash flow. One example is just to do a deal each and every month. That brings in a flow of cash and that is what I've been describing throughout this book.

But there are advanced cash flow opportunities as well. Here's an example for you. Don't worry if you don't fully understand these concepts. Just read it and get excited about the possibilities.

How I get ongoing cash flow from one deal. I tie up a deal for $35,000 with the seller but I want to sell the contract for $45,000. The property is worth $65,000. However, I'm happy to sell the deal for $45,000 and I have a hungry investor-buyer who only has $38,000 in cash right now but who really wants the deal badly.

So, I could do the deal for $3,000 down in cash to me today (remember my contracted price was $35,000 and my new buyer has $38,000 cash now) and then I'd simply finance the rest $7,000 at 10% over two years or less and make more on the deal.

So with this deal I created up-front cash and a monthly income, PLUS I will get a chunk of change in two years or less when the investor-buyer pays me off.

Yes you can create cash flow from deals. However, be aware that this is a tad more advanced and the majority of the deals will be done without any cash flow, especially in the beginning.

But remember! Your initial goal isn't cash flow at first. It's to do deals. You can always get more creative once you get experienced. At first, just get out there and do deals and I don't want these slightly-more-advanced concepts holding you back.

Get An Accountant

Earlier in the book I told you about the team you need to develop. I suggested that you mainly needed a virtual assistant, a mentor, and a lawyer.

In the beginning, that's all you really need. You can do your first few deals with those three people helping you. But eventually you will want to start thinking about what you're going to do with all of your money, and how you're going to handle your taxes – and perhaps consider if there are other ways you can manage your money to legally reduce the tax you pay.

This is where an accountant comes in. Find an accountant who is savvy with real estate investing. (I strongly advise this because non-real-estate-investing-savvy accountants might frankly not know enough about what you're doing to be able to help you).

Eventually, as you become more virtual in your wholesaling (and perhaps travel the world like I do) your accountant can take care of a lot of the financial side of your business – sort of like if you were outsourcing the Chief Financial Officer job of your business.

If you're not sure where to find an accountant who knows their way around a real estate investing deal, go talk to your local real estate investing clubs and see who they recommend. Make sure to interview a couple at least and find one you like to work with.

Again, I consider an accountant to be an advanced step in your virtual wholesaling because I just want you to do your first deal. Just get out there and get the deal done! I don't want you to get caught up in the very simple step of financials when you don't even have any income coming in.

The DM's Action Steps From This Chapter

Don't do these action steps until you have already set up your virtual wholesaling business. I don't want you getting caught up in these advanced details until the basics are done!

1. Segment your list of investor-buyers into some of the following categories:
    - By location
    - By type of deal preferred
    - By responsiveness
    - By experience

2. Find an accountant who understands real estate investing.

CHAPTER 12

THIS INVESTOR'S ACTION WILL CHANGE THE LIVES OF 8 PEOPLE (THAT HE'LL PROBABLY NEVER MEET)

Most chapters were written somewhere specific but this chapter is different. I want to highlight another real estate investor and show you how someone else is applying similar *virtual* real estate business principles like what I've been showing you in this book. And, I wanted to tell you about something amazing he's doing to change the lives of 8 people he'll probably never meet (I call it "Full Circle Giving". Keep reading to find out more).

A Virtual Real Estate Investing Success Story

Throughout this book I've showed you how you can build a real estate investing business so that it runs virtually, allowing you to do whatever you want in life (instead of having to work hard day-in and day-out in an office or on a rehab property).

And I love to share success stories about regular folks – just like you and I – who have taken relentless, massive action to achieve their dreams and run a virtual business.

The guy I'm about to introduce you to in this chapter is a rare breed. He's an action-taker who was willing to work toward his goals in life by becoming a real estate investor.

And what I also like about this story is that he demonstrates virtual real estate investing in action (even though he's not necessarily using the wholesale model that I've described throughout this book). And that's an important lesson I want to impress upon you – you don't have to follow what I describe in this book step-by-step. Instead, you can take what methods will work for you and customize them for your purposes.

As you read through his story, note how his business is becoming increasingly virtual. In particular, pay attention to the virtual systems he uses to run his business. And at the end of the chapter, I'll tell you about another amazing way he helped 8 people virtually.

Introducing Real Estate Investor Ronald Hoff

Ronald started investing in real estate in 2000 by buying a 3 bedroom, 2 bath row house at auction for $18,000. He put $5,000 into it and rented it out for $550 a month.

Since that first property, Ronald grew his real estate business by purchasing about 65 properties! He did wholesaling, rehabbing, buy and hold, lease option, owner financing, four private money deals as the lender, and a no-money-down commercial deal.

The DM says: **Great job, Ronald! Way to take relentless, massive action!**

Ronald Hoff's Creative Commercial Deal

Ronald told The DM about one of his deals, "*[My] commercial office building is my favorite property, because it is the most fun and rewarding. I purchased it in 2007 for no money down.*"

I'm going to share with you an interesting story about this commercial deal that Ronald calls his favorite property. Although it is not specifically a virtual deal, I want you to get excited to see how a little action and creativity (and a little hard work at the beginning) can be really rewarding.

Ronald tells us in his own words how he took massive action to close the commercial property for no money down, paying the full asking price and financing the entire purchase including closing costs. Note how Ronald creatively built up this business and, most importantly, made money by taking action.

First, Ronald explained how he got creative to acquire a commercial property…

180

"The owner owned it free and clear and wanted out. The majority owner was 80 years old and wanted to do other things. He no longer wanted to be a landlord, and told me he was a lousy one. I started thinking about how I would finance it.

I asked my lender what was the most they would finance, and the answer was 75 percent; therefore, I needed to come up with the remaining 25 percent. I asked the seller if he would take 15 percent back as a third position mortgage, and he said yes. My Realtor told me of a state program that would loan me the other 10 percent as a second position mortgage. I thought everything was ready and only the closing costs needed to be paid."

How Ronald Overcame The Challenges

Next, Ronald tells us about how he overcame challenges in the deal to make the deal happen…

"I never used government money prior to this deal and was not expecting it to delay the deal, but the government wanted a lien on all my rental properties in the state, which would force me to get government permission to sell any of them. Furthermore, we had delay after delay and finally learned that the paperwork was sitting on someone's desk who did nothing with it (because that person was more concerned with what they would be doing in a couple of months when the new governor was sworn in).

This almost killed the deal. Then I met with Realtor and the owner of the commercial property and I asked if the owner would take back 30 percent instead of 15 percent. This way, we don't have to deal with the state. At first he said no but a few days later he agreed and we closed the deal."

Once Ronald purchased the property, it was then time to make changes so the property could become an income-producing success story. Ronald says…

"I purchased the building on a Friday afternoon and on the same day posted a 30 day notice in the main lobby that all rents were going up 15 percent. Most of the tenants had no written lease

and were month to month; therefore, this was the only notice they needed to be given. I also followed that up with a written notice to all tenants.

I waited a couple of months before I posted my second lobby notice. This notice stated that all tenants will pay a prorated amount of the heating oil for the building based on the size of their suite. "

But the story doesn't end there! Every year for five years Ron has increased the gross income and net profit of the building, including (but not limited to) adding a fourth cell phone antenna lease this year. This no money down building has made a profit every year and currently nets Ronald $12,000 per month!

Way to go, Ronald! Ronald's story is an exciting one of massive action. And did you notice one of the important virtual real estate business I keep coming back to: Even though Ronald didn't use the exact wholesaling method I've described in this book, Ronald worked hard at the very beginning of the acquisition of the building and now he earns more in a month than many people earn in 3 to 6 months! Ronald is working smart, not hard. He is working on his business, not in his business.

How Is Ronald Running A VIRTUAL Real Estate Investing Business?

Virtual assistant: Ronald owns and manages 70 units and has a virtual assistant from the Philippines manage them for him. Using basic technology, she and Ronald are able to communicate with each other and she is able to do everything online except physically meet people at the properties or pick up rents.

He has 4 full-time virtual assistants and 1 part-time one, all of whom live and work from the Philippines. *"We use Skype, which has a local phone number. Nobody knows that the virtual assistants are not local,"* says Ronald.

His virtual assistants find properties and gather all the data Ronald needs in order to decide whether or not he wants to pursue a particular deal. They market his website and do all of his social media.

Ronald says, "*I have them to do whatever I can think of that can be accomplished online. I require all of them to turn in a daily report at the end of their work shift telling me hour by hour what they did. This makes it easy for me to review what they did and helps me with planning daily tasks for each of them.*"

"*They all have different strengths,*" he adds. "*I use them on tasks that they like and are well suited. I did not always do this and had fewer results. For example, Jeanne loves to talk; therefore, she is the one who talks to tenants, Realtors, buyers and sellers. When she gets someone ready to take action, she refers them to me. I close the deal. It works very well and saves me a lot of time. Janine loves SEO and social media. Therefore, she does all that stuff for me. Miguel is very good with graphics and is well rounded. He helps me in many areas.*"

Online technology for property management: Ronald runs his property management business almost entirely online using an online property management system. "*I think Buildium is the best*", says Ronald, who adds "*They are not paying me to say this. I tried a lot of software over the years and started using Buildium 4 years ago, and it has been great. Applications, credit and background checks, accounting, maintenance request, vendor management and anything else you can think of is done with this system. My virtual assistant can even send letters to tenants using Buildium, but we email most of the time.*"

Get Buildium by going to:
www.VirtualRealEstateMadeEasy.com/rent

Online technology to speed up filing: Ronald uses another online service to file in rent court. His virtual assistant handles the task. She even calls the sheriff to schedule a put out date when needed.

Using technology to build relationships and do deals: Ronald also bought a property from me on a webinar. But we've never met in person; the entire deal was done virtually: I was in Malibu (at the time), the deal was for a property in Atlanta, and he is in the D.C. area. So the entire deal is completely virtual.

Something Extra: Introducing "Full Circle Giving"

I believe in giving back. I frequently mentor students, I write books (and the proceeds are donated to charity), and I try to help people as much as I can. I don't say this to impress you. I tell you this because I want you to know that I'm a firm believer in giving back and I "put my money where my mouth is" and try to give back as often as I can.

Ronald and I did a virtual deal and because of that deal, Ronald's actions changed the lives of 8 people. Here's what happened:

I found a property using the virtual wholesaling techniques I've taught you throughout this book. Then on a webinar with some investor-buyers (of which Ronald was a participant), I offered the deal and I threw in a "Full Circle Giving" bonus: I told the webinar participants that if they bought the deal, the proceeds from the deal would be donated to a charity which would build a house for a family of 8 in Haiti.

So Ronald agreed to do the deal and it was an opportunity for both of us to give to a less fortunate family. Ronald's actions enabled a house to be built for a family of 8 in a country that has seen some hard times recently.

And it was all done with virtual real estate.

I just want to publicly thank Ron for the massive action and the opportunity to work with a true action taker.

CHAPTER 13

THE MOST IMPORTANT CHAPTER IN THIS BOOK

Santorini, Greece 3:21 PM
Writing from the house facing the caldera… breathtaking!

I'm writing this from deck overlooking the caldera we rented here in Santorini. It has an amazing view of the Santorini caldera (a volcanic crater)

Of the many places I've visited around the world, this is my favorite so far. Santorini is an amazing place. The whole city seems to be built out of pure white houses and they seem even brighter when reflected in the water of the Mediterranean. Everything is old and worn smooth. The weather always seems to be perfect. Santorini is a place I would come back to again and again.

As I sit here and sip my ouzo (hey, when in Greece, do as the Greeks do) I can't help but think of the one thing that got me here.

When people learn that I'm a world-traveling deal-maker, they wonder what the secret of my success is, and I'm often asked to speak about the secret of my success when I speak in front of groups of people (which I rarely do, due to the fact that it just doesn't fit into my schedule).

I could point to a number of reasons that I'm successful but there really is one thing that sets me apart from many of the people who aren't living out the lifestyle of their dreams.

Let me share that with you now!

Everything In This Book Hinges On This ONE Thing…

Throughout this book I've given details and steps and tips to help you become a virtual wholesaler. I've tried to leave no stone unturned to reveal to you exactly how you can go from a desire for success to running a real estate investing business that can potentially give you the success you want.

I've tried to instill the truth that working smart and digging your well before you are thirsty are vital ingredients to building a virtual wholesaling business that can be done from anywhere.

But everything I've written in this book hinges on the one lesson I'm about to teach you in this chapter.

When I'm asked about the secret of my success, and why others struggle to achieve their dreams, there are a lot of possible answers but I believe there is one key reason that my real estate investing business allows me to travel the world while other aspiring real estate investors toil away in their 9-5 jobs without ever achieving their dreams.

What is that secret? It's no secret at all, actually. I write about it quite a bit on my blog at MarkEvansDM.com. Simply put, the one secret that turns aspiring real estate investors into actual real estate investors (and then into successful real estate investors) is…

RELENTLESS ACTION

Successful virtual wholesalers take relentless action. They put down this book and then they immediately go out to implement what they've learned.

They follow the chapters step-by-step as if this book were a checklist of what they need to do. They do one thing after another until they've got a well-oiled virtual wholesaling business chugging away, with the objective of earning them daily cash and giving them the freedom to live the kind of life they want to live.

Ultimately, they take action – *massive action*!!! – to

become a successful virtual wholesaler.

Why Is "Relentless Massive Action" The Secret To Success?

So maybe you're scratching your head, wondering why "relentless massive action" is the secret to success.

Although there are many other important factors to being a successful virtual wholesaler, all of these factors hinge on just one thing: Actually *doing* something.

You can read and read and read about what you need to do but that doesn't make you a successful virtual wholesaler. The only thing that makes you a virtual wholesaler is getting a property under contract and then wholesaling that contract to an investor-buyer and getting paid!

Unfortunately, there are a lot of people who will read about how to make it happen and very few people who will actually do something. (And many will read and read and read but never take action – I call these folks "7-year newbies").

Virtual wholesaling isn't very hard and it doesn't take a lot of work if done correctly (as you've seen throughout the other chapters in this book) but if you want to succeed in this business, you need to move forward by taking action.

What Do I Mean When I Say "Take Relentless Massive Action"?

Let's say you're going on a vacation to the coast with your family. You book the hotel, you make sure everyone packs sunscreen, and when it's time to leave, you get into the car and you drive to your destination.

You don't just wake up one day and discover that you and your family have arrived at the beach. It doesn't work like that. You arrive at your vacation because of a series of smaller steps that you had to take. For example…

1. You decided where you wanted to go

2. You found a hotel deal online and you booked it

3. You marked your calendar and booked the time off of work

4. You packed your bags

5. You looked at a map to determine the best way to get there

6. You made sure the plants were watered and there was no leftover milk in the fridge

7. You put your bags in the car

8. Etc., etc.

You arrived at your vacation destination because of a series of actions that you took. If any of those steps were skipped, you probably wouldn't have a vacation (or you wouldn't have a very good vacation).

Although you tell people that you are going on vacation, what you are really doing is a series of activities that are all related toward going on a vacation. And once you're on vacation, you don't have to do anything – just enjoy the sun and the sand and the surf.

It's the same with virtual wholesaling. There are some activities you need to do to become a virtual wholesaler. As you've seen, all the activities are pretty simple and straightforward – but you still need to do them.

And the best part is (just like with any project), the hardest part is getting started. Once you get started and do the first couple of actions, everything else just starts to fall into place. You still take action but it becomes easier as you gain momentum from your first action. There's a law of physics that applies in business: "A body in motion tends to stay in motion". So once you start taking action, you're more likely to continue taking action.

So where do you start? Here's my suggestion: Visit www.VirtualRealEstateMadeEasy.com/va and post your project for a virtual assistant. It takes less than two minutes and you'll be on your way to building a virtual real estate business.

... did you do it? Not yet? Go do it now! What are you waiting for?

The Sad Truth About Why Some People Fail At Real Estate Investing

In the years that I've been a real estate investor, I've met a lot of people who aspire to become investors but who fail to take action. I've spent some time investigating the reasons and I'm listing them here for you to think about:

The feeling of being overwhelmed: Some people don't take action because they feel overwhelmed by the whole thing. They look at all the different components and it just becomes too much to fathom all at once.

They look at hiring a virtual assistant and putting a website together and creating ads and finding deals and assigning those contracts – although they might understand each part, it seems overwhelming to view it as a whole.

Virtual wholesaling is actually very easy to do but it can seem overwhelming if its various components are completely new to you.

If you find yourself almost overwhelmed by the world of wholesaling, and if it threatens to keep you from getting started, then here's what you need to do: Go back to Chapter 4 (Getting Started) and just do the steps in the chapter. Don't think about the other parts just yet.

Fear of failure or loss: Some people don't take action because they fear failure or loss. They don't want to put in the time and effort to start a virtual wholesaling business only to not make any deals (failure) or to lose their invested time (loss).

For example, they look at the small cost of a website and a virtual assistant and decide "I don't want to lose that money!" and so they fail to act. But what they don't realize is that their failure to act is actually costing them so much more in lost opportunity.

Fortunately, as I've shown in this book, there is very little required to be a virtual wholesaler. Although there is always risk in every business venture, virtual wholesaling minimizes the risks of failure and loss because virtual wholesalers don't do a lot of work and they don't use their own money to do deals.

If you want to become a successful virtual wholesaler, you can avoid the paralysis that comes with this kind of fear by remembering that virtual wholesaling doesn't "cost" a lot (of time or money or effort).

Fear of the unknown: Some people don't take action because they fear the unknown. That sounds strange but it's a pretty common reason for people not to take action. I see it happen so frequently! People look at the various pieces that make up virtual wholesaling and they get caught up in a detail instead of moving forward in general.

For example, they spend so much time wondering how a virtual assistant can help them, or how they'll ever find one and afford to hire one that they lose sight of how much easier a virtual assistant can be and how affordable one really is.

The most successful virtual wholesalers embrace the unknown. Whenever they have a question, they write it down and actively try to find an answer but (more importantly) they move forward anyway, trusting the process and confidently believing that they'll figure it out as they go.

If you follow the steps in this book, and if you have a mentor, you'll eliminate a lot of the unknowns. Take action and move forward. And just remember this: If fear of the unknown stopped people, we wouldn't be living in America because the early discoverers would have stayed in Europe, fearing for the unknown on the other side of the horizon.

Fear of success: Some people don't take action because they fear success. Okay, you might think I'm crazy by writing this. When I first heard that people fear success, I thought it was the strangest thing I'd ever heard. But as I met more and more aspiring real estate investors, I discovered that many people do fear success.

They fear success because it's different from what they are used to. In a way, the fear of success is the fear of change. Although someone dreams of a better life, they might be lulled into a false sense of comfort by the routines (and even the struggles) of their current life.

For example, someone might dream of golfing every day instead of having to go into the office, but they've gone into the office every day for the past twenty years and before that they went to college to get the degree to allow them to work at this job. And, a job gives the appearance of job security and a steady paycheck. So although their dream life is golfing, it's so different (and seemingly riskier) from the life they are used to.

Job security is just an illusion. Businesses are forced to let people go all the time. And that steady paycheck can vanish in a flash. (Besides, most people find that their paycheck doesn't quite cover everything they need to buy). On the other hand, a well-built virtual wholesaling business can not only bring in a steady, lucrative income, it can also get you the time-freedom you want to live the life of your dreams.

If you want to avoid being paralyzed by the fear of success, spend time daily imagining your perfect life and reminding yourself that it is within your power to achieve. And try to take a clear, analytical approach to the current "comforts" you have (like that "secure job" and "steady paycheck") and remember that your success feels so much better than the false sense of comfort you get from these other things.

Deciding to wait for something. Some people don't take action because they want to wait for something. It could be an arbitrary beginning date (like the start of next month or the start of next year) or it could be some other factor that lets them feel like they can make the switch (like waiting for the kids to go to college or waiting until there is a small amount of money saved up in the bank account).

For example, many aspiring real estate investors choose to avoid taking action because they're worried that the market is too soft or they avoid taking action because they don't have the money they think they need to get started (while many successful investors have started with little to no money and little to no credit – me included).

These waiting periods feel like you're taking action but they are delaying mechanisms. These delaying mechanisms put off the fears you might be feeling until another time. The "decision" is placed on something else to decide for you when you're ready to start. And, frankly, it gives you an excuse to avoid starting.

Find one or two people whose business methods and teaching style you like and follow them. If you try to follow everyone, you'll be so busy learning from many people that you'll never have time to take action.

If you want to become a successful virtual wholesaler, the best time to start is right this very instant. Don't wait until next month or next week or tomorrow. Do something right now.

What's The Best Way To Take Relentless Massive Action?

I've met a lot of people who avoid taking action. It's perfectly understandable because taking action can be disruptive and uncomfortable. But taking action is a necessary step to being successful.

Here's the best recipe for taking action:

1. Decide what you want to achieve (i.e. what you dream as your ideal lifestyle) and lock that firmly and vividly in your mind.

2. Decide what you can do this very instant to make it happen. Think of something measurable that you can do. I don't mean "try to find a virtual assistant", I mean break it down into a single step (such as "post a project for a virtual assistant at www.VirtualRealEstateMadeEasy.com/va" or "select an assistant and get in touch with them" or "give the assistant a list of things you need done").

3. Then do that one thing right this moment. Be focused; be determined; always remember why you're doing it.

4. If you're successful, great! If you stumble, try again. It's like the old saying: "Fall off the horse and jump back on".

5. Keep at it until that one step is done. Then go onto the next step.

Of course you can and should try to do more than one thing at once (heck, there isn't that much to do to become a virtual wholesaler) but the first couple of actions can be hard and this is a good recipe to get started.

Remember: You don't have to get it right you just have to get it going.

What Do You Have To Lose?

I always tell people that if they are afraid of losing money then here's what they should do: Set a worst-case cost (for example, $100.00) and try out what I'm suggesting. If they succeed, great! If they don't succeed, what's the worst thing that happened? They lost $100.00. But now at least they can say they tried it, instead of just thinking about it and wondering if it was for them!

Benefits Of Taking Action

There are many benefits to taking action. Of course becoming a successful virtual wholesaler is the ultimate reward but there are other benefits, too!

- You push yourself out of your comfort zone

- You are forced to think about your dream of an ideal life and what exactly it looks like (and how you'll achieve it)

- You gain momentum – each action builds momentum for the next (Small victories!)

- You get increasingly excited about your wholesaling business (that's a good thing!)

- You get increasingly excited about your future

- You build up an attitude of action which tends to attract other successful people to you

My Tips For Taking Relentless Massive Action

Know what your goals are. It's hard to move forward if you don't know what your goals are. Frankly, if you are approaching real estate investing with a wishy-washy attitude because it's something that your brother's friend's neighbor suggested and you thought you'd look into it then you're not ready.

You need to figure out what your goals are. You need to decide if you want to be a real estate investor and then how much you want to achieve financially and what steps you need to get there.

When you reach a big goal, break it down into several smaller goals. Real estate investing is extremely easy overall to those people who are doing it but it can seem strange (and therefore difficult or even impossible, especially in the beginning) to those who aren't investors.

It's easy to take a big goal and break it down into smaller goals. Just list the goal at the top of a piece of paper and list out all the things you need to do in order to achieve that goal. When you're done, you have a list of things you need to do.

My goal when I first started was to just do one deal (I didn't care how much I made I just wanted to go through the entire process) from start to finish, get it going and things will start falling into place with your action.

Get a mentor. A mentor is someone who is successful in the real estate investing field who can help you learn the ropes. A mentor will show you what to do, guide you through the tricky parts, and help you achieve success. A mentor can also hold you accountable when you want to move forward but when fear or procrastination holds you back.

Remember the mentor you choose cannot and will not do it for you but will be there to support you through your growth and assist you when you need assistance. Find one mentor that you really feel is where YOU want to be and get involved with them.

195

This was a changing point in my life! Without mentors, I don't know where I'd be today, but I know I wouldn't be writing this book.

If you're strapped for cash, sometimes a great first mentor can be a book or course that makes a ton of sense to you. This is a very affordable way to get going.

Schedule it. Life can be pretty busy so even if you want to act on a more successful life from real estate investing, it can be hard to figure out how to fit it in. But the best thing to do is to schedule it into your day. Estimate how long it will take you to do one action and schedule it into your day. Put it in your mobile device, set an alarm, and gather everything you need to act on that action when your alarm rings. This is so key! Don't try to do everything in one day. This will take time so focus on one action a day and get it done and celebrate the victory.

Better yet, do it right now: Even better than the above idea, go out right now and do one thing. Find something you can do right now to move forward as a real estate investor – even if it just takes 10 minutes of time. (In fact, that's a great way to think of any big project: Think of it instead as a series of small tasks). Just taking an action is key to getting going.

Just get started. People often find that a big, scary task is made easier simply because they broke through that initial barrier and got started. That's why I'm always telling you to take action even if I'm not specific on the action to take – mainly because the very action of taking action is going to have a huge, positive impact on your real estate business. This will give you some feedback from the market, like an ad only pulling in one lead instead of the five leads you thought you'd get. It's great to have something to measure against as you're growing your business. It's better to know with REAL results.

List all of the things that are keeping you from becoming a real estate investor today. Make a list and think of absolutely everything that is holding you back then, start addressing each one of those things. Some of the fears you might feel are best handled with research and talking to mentors. Not sure what to do first can also be handled by mentors. And the lack of funds can be solved with investors (just get more investor-buyers and you'll increase the likelihood of one of them doing a deal). And or maybe you need to look at the deals in the beginning that don't require money or credit. This is easily accomplished (and it's how I started). You'll find that many of the solutions you list turn out to be the first actions you should address.

The DM explains...

What keeps a lot of people from becoming real estate investors is the perception that they don't have the money to do it. Fortunately, with virtual real estate wholesaling, you don't need money to start. And, once you start, you can potentially get money pretty quickly... all you need are investor-buyers. So if you're concerned that you need money and if you listed "lack of money" as something keeping you from becoming a real estate investor then go out and find investor-buyers and your problem is solved!

List all of the things you would do if money and time were no object. By listing out all of the things you would do if money and time were no object, you create a motivational wish list for yourself. Looking at the list will remind you that you might not be able to achieve those desires in your present job but they are more likely to be achieved as a successful real estate investor. Let that thought inspire you to take a first step toward success.

The DM's Action Steps From This Chapter

1. Revisit your list of fears and challenges that are keeping you from becoming a virtual wholesaler. Add to the list.

2. Revisit all of the action steps in previous chapters. Have you completed each one?

3. Just take RELENTLESS Massive Action right now!

One final parting thought from The DM:

I've given you the tools and techniques that can make a big difference in your life. What happens next is up to you. It's decision time. You are on the cusp of an opportunity and what you do next is entirely up to you. It could be the start of something HUGE in your life.

Don't let another day go by without taking massive action. Take charge and do something big to totally transform your life.

You deserve it!

<u>APPENDIX</u>

In this next section, you'll find tools and resources to help you in your virtual wholesaling business.

Appendix 1: A survey that you can use to learn more about your investor-buyers.

Appendix 2: A guide to work with your list of fears and challenges (which you created throughout the book).

Appendix 3: A list of tools and technology you can use in your real estate investing business to help you run it virtually.

Appendix 4: All the forms you'll need in your real estate investing business.

APPENDIX 1

SURVEY

The survey questions below are part of a survey you can send out to investor-buyers to learn more about them, which helps you to send them deals that they'll really get excited about. It's a really simple survey of only 3 questions but these questions will reveal a lot about your investor-buyers.

Use SurveyMonkey.com to create a free survey and then send the link to your list.

To see what a survey looks like, view the link below (do not give out this link to your investor-buyers; create your own survey and give out that link).

Example survey: http://www.surveymonkey.com/s/D2STPTM

Here are the questions you can ask:

Basic details:
Name:
Email Address:
Phone Number:

Question 1:
What Type of Properties Are You Looking For?
- Single Family
- Multi Family
- Commercial
- Apartment Complex

Question 2:
What type of deals are you looking for?
- I'm looking for monthly cash flow properties (TURN KEY) - already rented
- I'm looking for rentals that need some work, where I can get for 50-70 cents on the dollar
- I'm looking for single family homes that I can do Options on (This requires around $3-$5k)
- I have cash and can close on any deals that make sense (Show me what you've got)

Question 3:
How many Real Estate Deals have you done to date?
Zero
1
2
3
4
5 or more

Just imagine the power of this survey. When someone answers these questions, you'll be able to tell at a glance what type of properties and deals to send and just how motivated and sophisticated they are. (Hint: The more motivated and sophisticated they are, the more likely they are to do deals with you).

APPENDIX 2

WORKING WITH YOUR LIST OF FEARS AND CHALLENGES

Throughout this book, you've been making a list of fears and challenges you have. The list included CHAPTER BY CHAPTER

If you look at this list, it can become almost overwhelming and might even keep you from wanting to move forward as a virtual wholesaler.

But it shouldn't cause you to think that way. Don't think of that list as a list of fears and challenges that will hold you back from virtual wholesaling. Think of that list as a list of questions that your mind needs to know and as soon as you answer those questions, you can move forward in your virtual wholesaling business.

Too many people don't bother writing down their fears and challenges and so they just feel some kind of weird, unknowable internal resistance to becoming virtual wholesalers even though they want to. But those who are serious about virtual wholesaling will write down the list and use that list as an educational to-do list. It's the list they'll take with them when they talk to their mentors or it's a list they'll take with them when they talk to a real estate investing lawyer or it's a list they'll use when researching.

This list isn't something that should slow you down. Instead, this list of fears and challenges should inspire you to cross each item off as you learn more about it.

It's like an exercise routine: When you exercise, you use heavy weights as resistance to build your muscles. As you get stronger, those weights seem lighter. What once felt like a heavy weight is now as light as a feather.

APPENDIX 3

LIST OF VIRTUAL TOOLS

Here is a list of virtual tools:

Email autoresponder
- www.DiscountEmailFollowup.com

Simple, fast websites
- www.VirtualRealEstateWebsites.com

Automated phone broadcasting
- www.CallToProfits.com

Free telephone system
- Google Voice: www.Google.com/voice
- Skype: www.Skype.com

Source for virtual assistants
- www.VirtualRealEstateMadeEasy.com/va

Find investor-buyer and deal leads
- www.VirtualRealEstateMadeEasy.com/sumo

Manage your real estate investing business
- www.PropFrog.com

Manage your real estate tenants
- www.VirtualRealEstateMadeEasy.com/rent

APPENDIX 4
FORMS

On the pages that follow, you'll find forms to help you every step of the way as a virtual wholesaler.

You can also find downloadable versions of these forms at www.VirtualRealEstateMadeEasy.com/forms.

Disclaimer: These are versions of the forms we use. However, it's important to note that each state is different so **you are responsible to ensure that these forms are legally binding for your situation**. Have a real estate investing attorney review the forms and make changes as necessary!

The forms are as follows:

1. **Deal At-a-Glance**: As its title indicates, this form allows you to quickly view all the information in a deal. Use this form to help you gather the information you need to do a deal. Provide this form to your virtual assistant to collect information. You can send this form to your investor-buyer, too.

2. **Letter of Intent**: This is the non-binding document that you'll get your seller to sign, which will help to lay out the details of the deal and will help you to gauge how serious the seller is.

3. **Option to Purchase**: This is the form you and the seller fill out for the property to be

bought from the seller. This is the contract you will "sell" to your investor-buyer.

4. **Assignment Agreement**: This is the form you complete when an investor-buyer pays you for the deal. This Option To Purchase form gives you the right to assign the purchase to someone else and this form indicates that you arc assigning the deal to someone (and it names the assignee – your investor-buyer).

5. **Purchase Agreement**: This is the form that is completed between the buyer and the seller to purchase the property.

DEAL-AT-A-GLANCE

Property Address:

Purchase Price:

Rehab Cost #1:

Rehab Cost #2:

Total Money In Deal:

Conservative Value:

Bedrooms:

Bathrooms:

Square Footage:

Schedule Closing Date:

Schedule Completion Date:

Lock Box Code:

Closing Attorneys:

Closing Attorneys Address:

Closing Attorneys Telephone:

Fax:

Closing Attorneys email:

Closing Attorneys website:

Potential Sale Price:

Potential Profit:

Copy in Back Office and Keep Hard Copy (If Applicable)

Deed?
Title Insurance?
Purchase HUD?

After Purchase of Property

Potential Sale Price:

Potential Profit:

If just wholesaling:
        $ Before Rehab:
        $ After Rehab:

After Rehab/Rent Out?

Electricity ON/OFF?
        If On, Who?
        If Off, Who?

Mowed Lawn Needed?

Any additional Lawn Maintenance needed?
        If yes, list:

Sale of Property

Executed Contract Received?

Contract sent to Attorneys office with projected Closing Date?

Contractors aware of Closing?

Closing Attorneys:

Closing Attorneys Address:

Closing Attorneys Telephone:

Fax:

Closing Attorneys email:

Closing Attorneys website:

Closing Attorney has copy of the following:

Deed?

Title Insurance?

Purchase HUD?

ID?

LLC Papers?

POA? (If Applicable)

Wire Instructions?

Buyers Name:

Buyers Address:

Buyers Telephone:

Fax:

Email:

Out of Pocket Expenses:

Postage:

Gifts to your seller and buyer

Wire Fees:

Letter Of Intent

I am the owner of real estate located at _____. It is my intent to enter into an agreement with _____ (hereinafter referred to as "Buyer"), on the following terms:

1. I will sign an Option agreement and related documents giving Buyer the legal right to lease and/or buy my property.

2. Sales price to be $_____ .

3. Length of time for Buyer to exercise Option to be _____.

4. Buyer has the right to lease my property for the monthly amount of $_____.

5. Seller will prepare all documents at his/her expense to finalize this transaction.

6. I understand it is Buyer's intention to find another buyer to purchase the property and assign the purchase contract for a fee. I agree to allow Buyer to put a sign in the yard, and advertise the property for sale.

This is a Letter Of Intent and is not binding. If these terms are acceptable to Buyer, he/she will prepare documents that are legally binding to be signed by the parties.

Signed this ____ day of _____, 20___ .
Seller _____
Seller _____

OPTION TO PURCHASE

THIS AGREEMENT made this _____ day of __, 20_
_____between,_____, (collectively referred to as
Optionor), and _____, collectively referred to as Optionee.

IN CONSIDERATION of the Optionee's payment of $_____, the
Optionor gives to Optionee the exclusive option, right and
privilege of purchasing certain real property located in
the City of ____, County of ____, and State of___, described as:

[Insert legal description]

Property Address:

This option is subject to the following terms and conditions:

1) Optionor grants Optionee the exclusive right to exercise this
option for a period commencing on the _____day of _____
_____, and terminating at 11:59 p.m. on the ___day of _____
20_____.

2) The purchase price of the property will be $_____.

3) Notice of election to Purchase shall be given by Optionee in
writing, and by first class mail, addressed to Optionor, at:
_____.

4) The option consideration is for the sole purpose of granting the
Optionee the exclusive right to purchase the subject property at the
stated price and terms.

5) This option to purchase shall apply to and bind the heirs,
executors, and administrators of the respective parties.

6) If the option is exercised, the related sale will be governed by a separate purchase contract executed by the parties concurrent with this Option.

7) Optionee has the right to multiple-list, advertise, rent or resell this property before or during this option period. In addition, Optionee has the right to freely assign this Option to a third party.

8) Time is of the essence in this agreement.

** Please let your local notary complete this page for you – it must be signed in their presence **

The parties have executed this agreement on the date first above written.

Optionor(s):

STATE OF   )
) SS.
COUNTY OF   )

The foregoing instrument was acknowledged before me this
_____20_____
by_____.

Notary Public,
My Commission Expires: _____

Optionee(s):

STATE OF   )
) SS.
COUNTY OF   )

The foregoing instrument was acknowledged before me this
_____20_____
by_____.

Notary Public,
My Commission Expires: _____

ASSIGNMENT AGREEMENT

This Agreement dated the _____ day of _____
is made between _____
(ASSIGNOR) and _____
(ASSIGNEE), regarding the property described as:

The property address is known as _____
(SUBJECT PROPERTY)

WHEREAS, _____
(ASSIGNOR) entered into a Purchase and Sales Agreement dated
_____, _____ with _____
_____ (SELLER) for the purchase of the
SUBJECT PROPERTY, and whereas ASSIGNOR wishes to
assign its rights and interest in the Purchase and Sales Agreement,
it is hereby agreed between ASSIGNOR and ASSIGNEE as
follows:

1. Assignment Fee. ASSIGNEE shall pay ASSIGNEE an
assignment fee of_____ U.S. Dollars. Assignment fee is
payable at close and shall not become due to ASSIGNOR until that
time and unless title to SUBJECT PROPERTY is delivered to
ASSIGNEE as per the terms of this contract and the Purchase and
Sale contract.

2. Down Payment. ASSIGNEE shall pay _____
U.S. Dollars of the Assignment Fee at the signing of this contract.
The Down payment is refundable only if the Seller does not
perform.

3. Closing Date. Closing is to take place on or before
_____.

4. Contract for Sale and Purchase Acknowledgement. ASSIGNEE accepts all terms and conditions of the original Contract for Purchase and Sale dated _____, in its entirety including all addendums associated with this transaction.

5. Hold Harmless. ASSIGNOR shall not be held responsible for the performance of the ASSIGNEE, and shall further be held harmless for any other circumstances arising from or in connection with the SUBJECT PROPERTY or the Purchase and Sales Agreement.

6. Non Performance Acknowledgement. ASSIGNEE has read Paragraph S under Standards for Real Estate Transactions on the original Contract for Purchase and Sale and hereby agrees to abide by its terms. ASSIGNEE agrees that the terms of Paragraph S shall apply to all deposits and down payments tendered under this Agreement

7. Ownership and Property Access Acknowledgement. At the time of this Agreement, ASSIGNOR owns a contract for Purchase and Sale of SUBJECT PROPERTY, ASSIGNOR does not own title to the SUBJECT PROPERTY. ASSIGNOR and affiliated associates do not authorize ASSIGNEE to enter onto the SUBJECT PROPERTY. ASSIGNEE holds ASSIGNOR and associated affiliates harmless from liability arising from ASSIGNEE entering onto the SUBJECT PROPERTY,

8. Limitation of Assignment. It is hereby acknowledged by ASSIGNEE that this Agreement to Assign Contract for Sale and Purchase and the original Contract for Sale and Purchase are not assignable by ASSIGNEE without the express written authorization of ASSIGNOR, authorization of which may be withheld for any reason by ASSIGNOR

9. Additional Disclosures and Acknowledgements.

     a. Inspection Report and Subject Property Condition. Assignor and affiliated associates make no warranty express or implied regarding inspection reports, subject property condition or value or other reports provided to ASSIGNEE by ASSIGNOR or third parties concerning this property. ASSIGNEE is advised to independently verify the accuracy of all information contained in reports concerning this property.

     b. Real Estate Brokerage Disclosure. ASSIGNEE acknowledges they are conducting a transaction dealing directly with ASSIGNOR for the purchase of the SUBJECT PROPERTY. ASSIGNEE Is not relying on or being represented by a real estate brokerage in this transaction.

     c. Affiliated Parties Disclosure. ASSIGNOR shall provide a statement of affiliated business arrangements. If any.

     d. Lead Based Paint and Energy Efficiency Brochures. ASSIGNEE acknowledges receipt of Lead Paint and Energy Efficiency Brochures.

     e. Entire Agreement This agreement constitutes the entire agreement and no modification 01 this Agreement shall be binding unless signed by the parties. No representation, promise or inducement not included in this agreement shall be binding upon any party hereto.

10. Additional Terms and conditions of this Agreement .are as follows:

AGREED AND ACCEPTED:

_____

ASSIGNOR	Date	ASSIGNEE	Date

_____

ASSIGNOR	Date	ASSIGNEE	Date

PURCHASE AGREEMENT

Dated this day of _____, 20___, (hereinafter "Buyer") and (hereinafter "Seller") hereby enter into this contract for the sale of property located at:

1. Purchase Price. The purchase price paid by Buyer in U.S. funds will be in the amount of $_____.

2. Terms.
(none if nothing inserted)

3. Contingencies.

> A) Environmental Inspection: (This paragraph not applicable if number of days not inserted.) Within _____ days after the acceptance hereof, Seller agrees to permit the Buyer, Buyers' lender and the qualified, professional environmental consultant of either of them to enter the premises to conduct, at the expense of the Buyer, an environmental site assessment. Buyer agrees to indemnify and hold Seller harmless from any injury or damage caused by such inspection. If such assessment is obtained and the consultant recommends further inspection to determine the extent of suspected contamination or recommends remedial action, the buyer, at Buyer's option, may notify the Seller in writing, within the above specified period, that the contract is null and void.

> B) Property Inspection: (This paragraph not applicable if number of days not inserted.) Buyer, at Buyer's expense, shall have ____days after the acceptance hereof to have the property and all improvement, fixtures and equipment inspected. Seller shall cooperate in making the property reasonably available for such inspection(s). Buyer agrees

217

to indemnify and hold Seller harmless from any injury or damage caused by such inspection(s). If Buyer is not satisfied with the condition of the property as disclosed by such inspection(s), Buyer may terminate this contract by delivering written notice of such termination to Seller within the time frame set forth in this paragraph.

C) Other Contingencies:

4. Title Insurance. Title insurance, if any, will be paid by Buyer at Buyer's expense.

5. Taxes. Taxes will be pro-rated to the date of sale and Buyer will be given a credit at closing for any and all unpaid real estate taxes together with any and all penalties and interest.

6. Deed. Seller will provide marketable title via a general warranty deed with release of title to Buyer or Buyer's designee free and clear of all liens unless otherwise noted (none if nothing inserted):

7. Legal Representation. Both parties have had an opportunity to seek legal counsel to advise them in this transaction.

8. Broker Representation. Both parties warrant that they are not represented in this transaction by a licensed real estate broker or agent and no funds from this sale will be paid to a licensed real estate broker or agent.

9. Closing Date. The parties agree that the closing will take place on or before the _____day of _____, 20____ at a title company of the Buyer's choosing. Buyer shall receive possession at closing.

10. Fixtures. This sale shall include any and all fixtures to the property including but not limited to: heating and air conditioning equipment, built-in appliances, curtains and curtain rods, attached carpeting, attached mirrors and lights, screens and storm

doors/windows, garage door openers, TV reception systems, outbuildings and all exterior plants and trees except as follows (none if nothing inserted):

11. Other. All representations and warranties of the parties are set forth in this contract and shall survive the closing. There are no representations, or agreements of the parties that have not been incorporated into this agreement.

12. Successors. This Agreement and all provisions hereof shall be binding upon and inure to the benefit of the parties hereto and their respective heirs, executors, administrators, legal representatives, successors and permitted assigns.

Signed on the date first written above.

BUYER   SELLER

_____   _____

"It is a paradoxical but profoundly true and important principle of life that the most likely way to reach a goal is to be aiming not at that goal itself but at some more ambitious goal beyond it."

- Arnold Toynbee

MORE FROM THE AUTHOR

Mark Evans DM,DN is committed to helping aspiring real estate investors start and grow virtual real estate investing businesses – a key step toward fulfilling their lifestyle dreams.

"The DM" (which is short for "The Deal Maker") is a prolific writer, communicating with real estate investors through his blog, email newsletter, and 5 bestselling books.

He is also a pioneer in the development of tools and techniques that are easy to use but allow real estate investors to work from anywhere without breaking a sweat or getting stuck in some of the traditional mistakes that are common in real estate investing.

On the following pages, you'll find a number of other books that The DM has written to help investors. They describe various aspects of real estate investing – from secret techniques and exclusive methods to essential mindsets and success factors.

You can take massive action by reading some of The DM's other writing and using the information to grow your real estate investing business.

Remember, it's all about taking massive action so move forward by getting the following resources...

TAKE ACTION...

GET YOUR COPY OF
THE REVERSE REAL ESTATE SYSTEM

Learn a virtually risk-free way to invest in real estate that is so powerful it is like having your own private ATM machine that spits out cash on demand!

Here are just a few of the benefits of the Reverse Real Estate System:

- No cash or credit needed!
- No license required!
- You can do this business anywhere!
- No Boss!
- No office required! (just need a kitchen table, fax, phone, computer)
- Never pick up a hammer again (Never do a rehab again)!
- You do not EVER have to buy a piece of real estate to make money!
- Discover how to put together your Million Dollar Team that will simplify your business and explode your profits at no cost!
- I show you how to create Multiple streams of revenue (this stuff is powerful and profitable)
- Never deal with those cocky bankers again. (I hate those guys too.) If you're not Bill Gates or Donald Trump, you're not getting a loan these days, especially with investment properties.

Take action by going to www.MarkEvansDM.com

TAKE ACTION...

GET YOUR COPY OF
GUERRILLA MARKETING FOR REAL ESTATE
INVESTORS: 101 WAYS TO MARKET YOUR BUSINESS

Learn the most effective marketing techniques from the one of the world's top marketing experts.

Jay Conrad Levinson is the creator of the Guerrilla Marketing brand and his techniques have helped millions of business owners around the globe.

Mark Evans DM,DN is a real estate investor who has pioneered virtual real estate wholesaling.

Together, these two best-selling authors show real estate investors...

- How to attract a lot of attention from prospective sellers and investor-buyers without the expense of traditional marketing methods
- The same tools and "Guerilla Marketing" techniques that the most successful real estate investors use every single day.
- Stunning advice and step-by-step how-to's that actually work, and have turned brand-new real estate investors into top-tier experts.
- Timeless advice that works online and offline without costing an arm and a leg!

Take action by going to www.MarkEvansDM.com

TAKE ACTION...

GET YOUR COPY OF
THE INSIDER SECRETS OF THE WORLD'S MOST SUCCESSFUL REAL ESTATE INVESTORS

Discover the shocking truth why 91% of "wannabe" investors fail and how to overcome this obstacle as if it never even existed... starting today. And, I'll even give you $3,472 worth of free bonuses to prove it!

- Discover how to double your income while also doubling your time off
- Learn how you can go from a $50,000 Fixer-Upper to a $100 Million Dollar Mansion
- Discover the huge pool of deals that you have access to right now and can profit greatly from – all while someone else is doing the work for you
- Discover how you can go from the Corporate World to Real Estate Investor in 1 year or less – all while not risking your own cash or credit
- Learn how a conventional Realtor went from $4 Million per year in sales to $100 Million per year in sales in one year's time with less work and more time to enjoy life...he reveals to you how you can do the same

Take action by going to www.MarkEvansDM.com

TAKE ACTION…

GET YOUR COPY OF
THE DONE FOR YOU LIFE: REAL ESTATE INVESTING THE WAY IT'S SUPPOSED TO BE

Best-selling author Mark Evans DM,DN reveals how real estate investing in today's day and age is done! This groundbreaking book introduced investors to the possibilities that they could invest in real estate using modern tools and techniques that made the opportunity easier, faster, and potentially more profitable!

In this book, investors will read…

- Where to get money to do your deals (including how to fix up your own credit if you want to use your own credit to invest in real estate.
- Where to find deals (and how to know if the deals are worth your time and effort before you sink too much time into each one!)
- How to plan for a profitable "exit" before you even start your deal, including what exit strategies you might consider.
- The ideal team that you absolutely need to build if you want to start your real estate investing on the right foot.
- … and so much more (including 9 money-wasting mistakes and how to engineer your ideal lifestyle!)

Take action by going to www.MarkEvansDM.com

TAKE ACTION...

CONNECT WITH MARK EVANS DM,DN

You can connect with The DM,DN in the following ways:

1. Bookmark his website, www.MarkEvansDM.com, to read The DM's latest real estate investing ideas and techniques (plus tips and tricks you won't learn anywhere else!). Don't forget to comment on his blog posts when you have an idea or question you'd like answered.

2. While you're on his site, sign up for his exclusive newsletter where you'll hear about opportunities to work with The DM, plus you'll learn great tips about real estate investing!

3. Use this special link if you have a question about this book, or about doing a deal with The DM, or to find out how to book The DM to speak about running a virtual business: www.replytomarkevansdm.com.

Take action by going to www.MarkEvansDM.com